Black Men Rock!

10 Keys To Empower Black Men To Live Extraordinary Lives!

By

Coach Michael Taylor

*Transforming The World
Once Man At A Time!*

Published by Creation Publishing Group
www.creationpublishing.com

© 2012 Michael Taylor

ISBN: 978-0-9641894-8-5 (paperback)
ISBN: 978-0-9641894-9-2 (hardcover)
LCCN: 2012924234

All rights reserved. No part of this book may be used or reproduced, stored in or introduced into a retrieval system, or transmitted in any form or by any means without the express written consent of the Publisher of this book.

Published and printed in the
United States Of America

Outline

Acknowledgements	v
Introduction	vii
My Story	xiii
Key #1: Know Thyself	1
Key #2: Develop A Spiritual Connection That Nurtures Your Soul	21
Key #3: Develop A Positive Attitude	35
Key #4: Make Relationships Top Priority	51
Key #5: Develop A Positive Support System	71
Key #6: Do Not Buy In To The Negative Media	79
Key #7: Take Care Of Your Physical Body	93
Key #8: Manage Your Finances	101
Key #9: Embrace Technology	115
Key #10: Be In Service To Your Community	125

Acknowledgements

First, foremost, and always, I must acknowledge the energy and intelligence that created and is still creating this amazing Universe. This energy and intelligence I choose to call God, and without question it is the source of my creativity and passion, and I acknowledge it as my Source.

To my Source, I simply say thank you!

Thank you for the courage to pursue my dreams and the persistence to bring them to fruition. Thank you for teaching me to listen to my own inner wisdom, which I now recognize as your still, small voice within me. Thank you for the gifts of writing and speaking, which allow me to share my insights and knowledge with others to support them in connecting with their own inner wisdom. And thank you for the vision of a united humanity in which every human being awakens to their true essence and discovers their own individual gifts and talents and uses them to make the world a better place.

I commit my life to being in service to your divine plan, and I accept the responsibility of shining your light around the world to remove as much darkness as I possibly can. Thank you for expressing through me as me. I am forever indebted to your unconditional love and acceptance. I love you more than love!

~~~~~~~~~~

I would like to say a special thank you to my elementary school teacher, Mrs. Bussey, who instilled in me a love for learning and the belief that I was an intelligent young Black man with unlimited potential. Thanks for believing in me!

I must also thank my mom, who taught me to be an optimist, not through her words, but through her actions. No matter what challenges my mother faced, she always maintained a positive attitude. I love you, Mom! Your positive attitude definitely rubbed off on me. You always told me to reach for the stars!

To my wife Bedra, who loves me unconditionally and has a heart as big as Texas, I simply say thank you for loving me for who I am, not what I do. You have accepted me for the man that I am, and your belief in me has definitely made it easier for me to pursue my dreams. Kiss Kiss, Mrs. B! I Love You!

And last, but definitely not least, I want to acknowledge all the Black men around the world who may have given up on their dreams and do not believe that it is possible to live an extraordinary life. Know that it is possible, no matter what your current circumstances might be. If I can go from a high school dropout to an entrepreneur, author, motivational speaker, radio show, and television host, then I know without question you can also live your dreams. It may not be easy, but I can assure you that it will be worth it if you trust your heart and pursue your passions. This book is written to assist you on your journey.

Good luck!

Introduction

When I was approximately 10 years old, I remember a conversation I had with my grandfather about race. I'll begin by letting you know that he only had an 8th grade education, yet he was one of the smartest men I've ever known. As I reflect back on all of the books I've read, the seminars I've attended, and the audio programs I've listened to over the years, I realize that the most important lessons about life I learned from him, and he was by far my greatest teacher.

He was a deeply religious man who never preached or tried to tell me what to believe about God, but he always made sure that I understood the importance of believing in a power greater than myself. He was definitely a man of deep faith with a deep spiritual connection to the God of his understanding.

During our conversation, I asked him why God allowed Black people to suffer so much. As a child, I noticed the atrocities inflicted upon Black people, and I really wanted to understand why God allowed them to happen.

As he looked at me with his loving, caring eyes, he could tell that I was a little upset with the question, and he caringly embraced me and instilled his deep wisdom.

"First of all, Michael, you must understand that God never makes mistakes. It's difficult for us to truly know God's purpose for things sometimes, but I trust in God's plan, and I know that ultimately His plan is always perfect. Since I believe in God's perfect plan, I must accept it, even when I can't fully understand it. I believe God has a perfect plan for Black people, and though it may appear that God has deserted us, He hasn't, and He is always there for us.

"The key is for you to recognize that you must always play the hand that is dealt you. If God made you Black, then that is the hand God dealt you, and it is your responsibility to play that hand. Remember, God does not make mistakes! The most important thing to remember is that your success depends on how you play the hand that you were dealt. Never question the hand; simply learn to play it to the best of your ability."

If I had to sum up the key to my own success, I would sum it up with those words of wisdom from my grandfather: "You must always play the hand that you were dealt, and if God made you Black, then that is the hand God dealt you!"

Fortunately for me, I embraced these words of wisdom at a very young age, which has allowed me to overcome some seemingly insurmountable obstacles and build the life of my dreams. As a result of accepting this truth, I can say with absolute certainty and conviction that as a Black man, I have never felt that the color of my skin was a disadvantage. In no way have I ever felt or believed that being Black was a negative or bad thing. I have always believed that it was an asset, not a liability, and this way of thinking has empowered me to accomplish some pretty amazing things in my life. I have simply played my hand to the best of my ability.

As I see it, one of the greatest challenges we have as Black men is to recognize that being Black is not a disadvantage. This does not mean that racism, discrimination and a myriad of other challenges don't exist; it simply means that you have to accept the hand you were dealt and learn how to play that hand to the best of your ability.

There are some people who believe that Black men are an endangered species and that there is nothing that can be done to stop the eradication of the Black male species. I, however, do not believe this nonsense, and it is my belief that Black men are doing better than ever and that the future is extremely bright for Black men. I do not deny the challenges; I simply believe that there has never been an obstacle placed before Black men that we haven't overcome.

When I think about things like slavery, discrimination, prejudice, ignorance, and the negative media images of Black men, I don't feel victimized; I personally feel inspired and empowered. I feel inspired that I belong to a group of men that epitomizes faith, determination, perseverance, persistence, and courage. I feel inspired because I recognize that despite all of the obstacles placed in front of us, we have found a way to thrive and flourish in a country that seemed to do everything in its power to keep us from succeeding; therefore, I stand proud as a man who happens to be Black, and I believe the best is yet to come.

Our challenge is to change our mindset from that of victim to that of victor. We Are Not Victims! Without question, we have been victimized, but that does not mean that we have to remain victims because what happens to you isn't as important as what you do with what happens to you. Instead of feeling victimized, recognize that you are victorious despite what may have happened to you if you choose to have a victorious mindset.

We must embrace the idea that we are filled with unlimited potential and that it is our responsibility to access our innate magnificence and personal power. The time has come for us to begin empowering and supporting each other in reaching our full potential and to be willing to share our wisdom with others to help them overcome their own struggles. "Reach one and teach one" must become our motto, and when we do this, we will begin to see the eradication of the majority of the social ills that currently plague our communities.

And most importantly, it's time for us to recognize that the "struggle" is over. Being caught in the "struggle" is an antiquated mindset that will keep you trapped in mediocrity and the victim mentality. Yes, there are still challenges, but the doors of opportunity are wide open for those of us who are willing to walk through them and live the life of our dreams. Struggle is a choice. My suggestion is that you simply choose not to believe that your life has to be a struggle, and it won't be.

This also means that we must eliminate the idea that society and white people are conspiring against us. It is my contention that the overwhelming majority of white people are definitely not racist and conspiring to keep us down. Most of them are supportive and caring and open-minded and want the same things that we do. We want to love and be loved, we want to feel that we make a difference, and we want peace of mind and a sense of purpose. Isn't that what you really want out of life?

Of course it is; it's what all human beings strive for. No longer can we blame white people or society for us not accomplishing these things. If you want to be loved, to make a difference in the world, and to have inner peace and a sense of purpose, it is completely up to you. You simply have to believe that you're capable of attaining these things and then get started in making them happen.

As we move into 2013, let's declare that it is the year of infinite possibilities. Make a commitment to yourself that you are going to live an extraordinary life and that there is nothing that can keep you from it. Know that you already have everything you need to make this a reality for yourself but that it is definitely going to take a considerable amount of effort on your part. It may be difficult, but I can promise you that it will be worth it.

My commitment to you is to share my experience and wisdom to support you on your journey. The good news is that you do not have to do this alone. There are lots of other men and women who will support you if you are willing to seek the support.

This book is my attempt to share some wisdom and knowledge with you that can encourage and motivate you to create your best life ever. If I can overcome seemingly insurmountable obstacles to live an extraordinary life, then I know that you can, too. You just have to be willing to take the first step, and I believe if you are reading this right now, you have done just that. Congratulations on taking the first step to living an extraordinary life!

I look forward to seeing you along the way!

Never forget: "You must always play the hand that you were dealt, and if God made you Black, then that is the hand God dealt you, and rest assured that it is a positive hand!"

No matter what color you are, it's perfect. Just play the hand you were dealt to the best of your ability, and you, too, will live an extraordinary life!

Coach Michael Taylor

My Story

I was born in the inner city projects of Corpus Christi, Texas. My mother was a single parent with six kids, and by society's standards, we would have been considered extremely poor. But what we lacked in finances, we made up for with motivation from a woman who refused to allow our financial situation to dictate our future. From a very early age, my mother instilled in me a sense that anything was possible. She always told me that I was 100 percent responsible for succeeding and that I should never use my race or our current financial situation as an excuse for failure.

She always told me that the key to my success was my intellect. She would tell me that I was extremely smart and if I applied myself, I could do anything I wanted to do. She said that the key to my success was a good education and that it was imperative that I received this education if I truly wanted to be successful.

At the age of six, my oldest sister became extremely ill, and my mother had to take me, my brother, and my sister to live with our father. My parents had divorced while I was extremely young, so I didn't really have any memories of him. When we arrived at my father's house, I learned that he lived with his mother, who turned out to be the grandmother from hell.

She was a raging alcoholic who hated my mother and would take every opportunity to tell me what a no good woman my mother was. When I would defend my mother by saying that she wasn't, she would go into this violent rage and take it out on me with verbal and physical abuse that no child deserved to experience. After several violent outbursts, I learned to keep my mouth shut and not talk back to her, even when she would talk badly about my mother. I'm not sure which hurt worse, listening to her bad mouth my mom or the physical beatings, but I decided that it was in my best interest to stop the beatings whenever I could, so I learned to keep my thoughts and feelings to myself.

The good news is that my grandfather was the complete opposite. He was a quiet, loving man who didn't talk much, but when he did it was usually pretty profound. I immediately became attached to him, and he became like a big brother to me. My fondest memories of him are when we would sit out in the yard amongst a variety of farm animals and talk about all sorts of topics. One of our favorite places for conversation was sitting on milk crates around a table made from one of those big spools that electric companies use to hold electrical cable. At this makeshift table, he would share his words of wisdom with me while chickens, ducks, and goats walked around us and sometimes seemed as though they were listening in on our conversations.

One of the most influential persons of my young life was my elementary school teacher, Mrs. Bussey. She was a loving woman who was extremely friendly and would give me hugs as soon as I got to school. Whenever she would hug me, it felt as though I were hugging Santa Clause because I could feel her love as she embraced me. She was aware of the physical and verbal abuse I received at home, and she made it a point to let me know that she cared about me and would do anything she could to make sure that I succeeded in school. She told me that I could accomplish anything I wanted in life if I would apply myself and make good grades. As a result of her encouragement, I was a straight A student that thrived academically and actually loved going to school.

After approximately 7 years (which I called my seven years of hell), my mother was able to reunite our family, and she allowed us to move back to my hometown. She hadn't planned on bringing us home at the time, but during our drive home from a visit to an amusement park, she looked in the rearview mirror and noticed I was crying. She asked me why I was crying, and I told her that I really hated living with my grandmother and that I wanted to go back home with her.

My brother and sister also said how much they hated being there and that they also wanted to go back to our hometown. As my mother looked at me through her rearview mirror and watched the tears continuously rolling down my face, she made the decision to not take us back. She knew how difficult it was going to be for her to raise all of us, especially with my sister's medical bills, but she said she would find a way.

I remember the feeling of joy I felt as she turned the car around and headed back to our hometown. My tears of sadness turned to tears of joy as we headed home. My seven-year nightmare with the grandmother from hell was over, and now it was time for me to move to the next chapter of my life.

When we arrived back in Corpus Christi, it was somewhat of a culture shock. My mother was living in some really nice housing projects, with lots of other children to play with and playgrounds and basketball courts. It was quite different from the farming environment I had grown accustomed to, but I have to admit, it was a lot more fun having friends to talk to instead of hanging out with the farm animals.

The good news was that I gained lots of friends and no longer felt alone in the world; the bad news was that in order for me to make and keep friends, I gave up on excelling academically because it was more important for me to have friends than it was to get good grades.

My friends meant everything to me. For the first time in my life, I had people I trusted and could confide in. My friends accepted me unconditionally, and I would do anything to make sure I maintained their friendship; unfortunately, this loyalty led me to skipping school and not taking my education seriously.

As I grew into my teen years, I became extremely bored with school and decided that I would take a chance and try to make it on my own. I decided to drop out of high school in the eleventh grade because I went to a seminar in which the facilitator convinced me that I could become rich selling vacuum cleaners.

Of course, my mother objected to this irrational decision, but I had made up my mind, and there was no one who could convince me to change it.

It was definitely a bad decision, and after six months and not selling a single vacuum cleaner, I finally realized how bad the decision really was. Fortunately for me, my mother was still supportive, and she encouraged me to go back to school and get my diploma. I promised her that one day I would, but what I needed to do first was find a job so that I could get on my feet and move out on my own.

At the age of 18, I landed a full-time job with a building supply company that allowed me to get my first apartment. I cannot begin to describe the feeling of freedom and accomplishment I felt when I moved in. The feeling only motivated me more to want to take the next step and move into my own house. I knew that I could not settle for just an apartment; I wanted to experience home ownership.

For the next four years, I worked extremely hard and climbed the corporate ladder to become the youngest manager in the history of the company. As a result, I was able to fulfill my dream of owning my own home at the age of 23.

So there I was, living the American Dream. I had the house, the wife, the 2.5 kids, and everything appeared to be perfect. But within the span of approximately 6 ½ years, my dream turned into a nightmare as I went through a divorce, bankruptcy, and foreclosure and lost everything.

During this time, I entered into a deep state of depression, and I even considered taking my own life. But something in me decided that I wanted to live, and I reached deep within myself and made a commitment to get my life back on track.

After approximately 15 years, I was able to put my life back together, and right now I can honestly say that I am living what I consider to be an extraordinary life. I am living my dream of being an entrepreneur, author, speaker, radio, and television host. I have been happily married for more than ten years, and I am in excellent health and have wonderful friendships and relationships with my children.

Was it easy? Absolutely not! But I did it! And if I can do it, you can, too!

I share these things not to brag, but to let you know that it is absolutely possible for any man to live an extraordinary life. But most importantly, it is definitely possible for Black men to live extraordinary lives also. With all of the negative media stories surrounding Black men, it's easy to see why some of them fall victim to those negative stereotypes and behaviors. But I fervently believe that the future is extremely bright for Black men, and I wanted to share the lessons I've learned that have allowed me to live my dreams in hopes of inspiring others to do the same.

If I can go from being born in the inner city projects of Corpus Christi, Texas, to a single mother with six kids, and then be subjected to extreme child abuse for 7 years by the grandmother from hell and survive that situation, and then drop out of high school yet still be able to climb the corporate ladder and live the American Dream, and then watch that dream turn into a nightmare and endure a divorce, bankruptcy, foreclosure, and a deep state of depression, and then ultimately rebuild my life to become a life coach that empowers others to live the life of their dreams, don't you think you can overcome your own personal challenges and create the life you deserve?

In my opinion, there is no excuse for you not to live your dreams. There is no excuse for you not to live an extraordinary life! You have everything you need within you right now to do so. All you have to do is make a conscious choice that you want to change your life and then come up with a vision for how you want your life to turn out. Then commit to that vision and do not quit until you fulfill it.

It is definitely not going to be easy, but rest assured, it will be worth it. You can do this; I know that you can.

This book should be used as a guide to help you do so. It contains the 10 keys of success that I have used to live my version of an extraordinary life. You will have to define 'extraordinary' for yourself, but if you follow these ten keys, I know that you can create the life of your dreams.

Good luck!

Coach Michael Taylor

"The real power behind whatever success I have now was something I found within myself - something that's in all of us, I think - a little piece of God just waiting to be discovered."
Tina Turner

Key #1: Know Thyself

One of my all time favorite movies is "Guess Who's Coming To Dinner", with one of my all time favorite actors, Sidney Poitier. In the movie, Sidney plays a Black doctor whose wife and son are killed in an accident. He then meets and falls in love with a woman who happens to be white and decides he wants to marry her. He decides to go to his girlfriend's parents' house to introduce himself and get her father's approval, and he also invites his parents to be there so they can get to know each other. The surprise is that her parents didn't know he was Black, and his parents didn't know that she was white, hence the title "Guess Who's Coming To Dinner".

My favorite scene in the movie occurs when Sidney and his father are having a conversation about whether or not he should marry the woman. In the conversation, his father is attempting to put a guilt trip on him by saying that he is indebted to him for working so hard as a mail carrier and that he should not marry a white woman because he owes his father for sacrificing so much of his life for his son.

All of a sudden, Sidney looks at his father directly and says:

"No, you said what you had to say. You listen to me. You say you don't want to tell me how to live my life, so what do you think you've been doing? You tell me what rights I've got and haven't got and what I owe to you for what you've done for me? Let me tell you something. I owe you nothing. If you carried that bag a million miles, you did what you were supposed to do because you brought me into this world, and from that day you owed me everything that you could ever do for me, like I will owe my son if I ever have another. But you don't own me. You can't tell me when or where I'm out of line or try to get me to live my life according to your rules. You don't even know what I am, Dad. You don't know who I am. You don't know how I feel, what I think, and if I tried to explain it the rest of your life, you will never understand. You are thirty years older than I am. You and your whole lousy generation believes the way it was for you is the way it's got to be, and not until your whole generation has laid down and died will the dead weight of you be off our backs. You understand, you got to get off my back. Dad, Dad, you're my father. I'm your son. I love you. I always have, and I always will, but you think of yourself as a colored man. I think of myself as a man. "

There are two sentences in this dialogue that really stand out for me.

1. "You and your whole lousy generation believes the way it was for you is the way it's got to be, and not until your whole generation has laid down and died will the dead weight of you be off our backs. You understand, you got to get off my back."
2. "You think of yourself as a colored man. I think of myself as a man."

The first sentence shares a sentiment that I really resonate with. Unfortunately, too many people get trapped in their past and believe that the way it was for them is the way it has to be for everyone else. From a Black male perspective, I have heard lots of people use this way of thinking as an excuse for failure. Whenever I hear people talk about how difficult it is for Black men to succeed, I understand that they are trapped in this mentality. Just because Black men experienced racism and discrimination in the past does not necessarily mean they will experience it in the present.

And even if they do experience it, they can choose to react differently today than they did fifty years ago.

The key is to accept the fact that your past does not have to dictate your future and that the key to your success lies in how you deal with situations in the present moment.

Metaphorically speaking, the dead weight that he is speaking about is an antiquated way of thinking. When an older generation refuses to let go of the past and continues to pass on their beliefs to the next generation, progress cannot be made.

Albert Einstein said it best when he said, "All of the problems of a society cannot be resolved with the same level of thinking that created them in the first place." In order for us to move forward, we must let go of the past way of thinking and embrace some new ways of thinking that allow us to come up with new solutions to the challenges we face. This is how we remove the dead weight off our backs.

The second sentence is probably the most important sentence of the whole movie: "You see yourself as a colored man. I see myself as a man."

Collectively speaking, I believe too many Black men are facing an identity crisis. On one hand, they are faced with maintaining their ethnic identity; on the other hand, they are trying to break free from the negative media stereotypes of what a Black man is supposed to be like.

If you turn on the television or watch movies or even read some magazines, you should recognize that the media generated perception (MGP) is that Black men are uneducated, violent, sex-crazed, lazy, irresponsible, baggy pants wearing gangstas with no morals or direction; thereby, too many of our men try and imitate this misperception because they believe that's what Black men are supposed to be like.

On the other hand, you have Black men who know that these images are not who they really are. They are intelligent, caring, ambitious, thoughtful men who know right from wrong, yet they want to fit in with the mainstream media and they feel left out if they don't emulate what the media generated perception says they should be like.

So what do we do to support Black men and keep them from falling victim to the negative media generated stereotypes? I believe the answer lies in Sidney Poitier's last statement: "You see yourself as a colored man. I see myself as a man."

In order to support Black men and keep them from falling victim to the negative media stereotypes, we must empower our men to discover who they really are and recognize that they are men who happen to be Black, not just Black men.

Let me clarify what I mean.

Socrates said it best when he uttered his famous words, "Know Thyself." This philosophical reference points to the idea that every human being has access to a part of himself/herself that is known as the higher self. This higher self has nothing to do with ethnicity, but is actually an aspect of our divinity.

What Sidney was saying in his quote was that he recognized that he would not see himself simply as a color, but more importantly as a man who knew who he was and was connected to his higher self. He knew that as long as he accepted the label of "colored", he would be shackled with the limitations of what it meant to be a colored man. He didn't deny his ethnicity; he simply affirmed his divinity. It did not mean that he was ashamed of being a colored man; it meant that he recognized that the source of his true power came from within. This is why it is so important to teach that we are men who happen to be Black rather than just Black men.

I remember a conversation in which I said that I did not relate to being called African American. I said that I related more to being called Black because it wasn't about my skin color; it was about my experience. When I think about the civil rights movement and the personal experiences I've had with racism and discrimination in America, these were Black experiences that had nothing to do with Africa. So for me, defining myself as a Black man feels more authentic.

But the men I was having the conversation with accused me of being a sell out and not understanding the significance of acknowledging my ethnic heritage. Their argument was that I needed to acknowledge that my DNA originated from the African continent and that I should be proud of this fact.

To which I replied, "You can see yourself as African American if you choose. I choose to see myself as a man who happens to be Black, and I am comfortable with that choice. I refuse to allow anyone to tell me what I should think, what I should believe, or how I should act. I am my own man, and I march to the beat of my own drummer."

We must understand that we are no different than any other group of men. We are not less than or better than other men. We are diverse in our thinking and our actions. We should not be placed in a "Black box" and forced to believe something or act a certain way simply because our culture says its what we're supposed to do. We must learn to "Know Thyself" and base our actions on our own thoughts, feelings, and beliefs. Our goal should be to connect to and listen to our higher self and allow it to guide us, not our culture or society. We must take Shakespeare's advice: "To Thine Own Self Be True!

So how do we get Black men to embrace this idea and make the commitment to "Know Thyself"? How do we get men to change?

Contrary to popular belief, you can teach an old dog new tricks; in other words, every man has the ability and the capacity to change his behavior if he so chooses. It does not matter what color he is or how old he is. It does not matter what religion he practices or what school he graduated from. It does not matter if he's from the inner city or the Hamptons. If a man truly wants to change, he has the capacity to change. The problem isn't a man's ability to change; the problem is that most men simply aren't willing to change.

So the million dollar question is this: "Why is it so difficult to get men to change?"

To answer this question, I would like to share a story with you that will serve as a metaphor for why men are so resistant to change.

Have you ever heard the story of how they train elephants? When an elephant is first born, the trainers use extremely huge and heavy chains to chain them to the ground. No matter how hard the baby elephant pulls on that chain, they simply can't break free. The elephant will pull and pull until it reaches a point of exhaustion, and then it realizes the futility in its efforts and eventually stops pulling. As the baby elephant grows up, they begin using smaller and smaller chains on him, and the elephant continues to pull, but the elephants know from previous experience that no matter how hard they try, they simply cannot break free. By the time the elephant is fully grown, it only takes a small nylon rope to keep him imprisoned, a rope so small that it would only take a minimum amount of effort by the elephant to break free - yet he won't do it. He simply stays trapped by an obstacle that is so small that it baffles the human mind that an animal that weighs several tons is being held back by a rope that would take very little effort on the elephant's part to break free.

So why won't he do it? Why does he choose to stay imprisoned by such a small obstacle? The answer is simple: he does not "believe" that he can break through the obstacle, based on his previous conditioning.

This is the primary reason most men are so resistant to change. They simply do not "believe" that they can change. Too many men fall victim to the belief that "that's just the way that I am", and they refuse to be open-minded enough to see themselves from a different point of view. They remain locked in a prison in their own mind that keeps them from transforming their lives into something better.

Over the past 15 years, I have lectured, coached, and participated in many seminars that support men to embrace change and become authentically happy with themselves. I have watched men who were tough and rigid become loving and sensitive. I have witnessed men go from being a sleazy womanizer to a monogamous, loving, and caring husband. I have watched men be transformed from deadbeat dads to nurturing, caring fathers, so I know beyond the shadow of a doubt that any man can change if he makes the commitment to himself and wants to change.

So now I want to take this opportunity to share the top five reasons I believe some men refuse to change.

1. Fear
2. Pride/Shame
3. Unwillingness to say, "I Need Help!"
4. Unwillingness to say, "I Don't Know!"
5. Cultural conditioning

Fear

Most men may not admit it, or they may not be aware of it, but fear is the root cause of a man's unwillingness to change. We are afraid of change, afraid of failure, afraid of uncertainty, afraid of looking bad or being judged, afraid of success, and afraid that we are not capable of change. Our culture has conditioned us to believe that feeling fear is definitely not okay, so we repress and deny our fears, and then they show up in unconscious ways. For example, a man may appear to be tough and insensitive, when in reality he is afraid of getting hurt, so he uses being tough as a mask to hide his fear. Men devise myriad ways to deny their fears, but it isn't until they address them that they can truly change their lives.

Pride/Shame

Shame can be a powerful motivator, but unfortunately it robs a man of his self-worth and self-esteem. When a man is driven by shame, he feels that he is somehow inadequate or defective, so he tries to compensate by doing things that make him appear to be adequate and capable. Many high achievers are driven by shame. It can be a coping mechanism to temporarily help a man feel good about himself, but unfortunately it is short-lived because no matter what he accomplishes, he still feels inadequate. If a man is gripped by shame, he will definitely be resistant to change.

Unwillingness to say, "I Need Help!"

I honestly believe that the three most difficult words for a man to say are "I Need Help!" Regrettably, if a man is unwilling to admit he needs help, he obviously can never expect to change. Most men will not admit that they need help until they experience some traumatic event in their lives. By then, it is often too late, and men will be forced to change after losing all they hold dear.

Unwillingness to say, "I Don't Know!"

The twin brother of "I Need Help" is "I Don't Know!" It is another one of those simple phrases that men have so much trouble saying. By declaring that we don't know, we open the door to know, and it isn't until we admit that we don't know that we can truly learn and know something new. If a man is going to change, he must be willing to begin by saying, "I don't know!"

Cultural Conditioning

Just like the elephant in the story above, we are conditioned by our upbringing and we carry an enormous amount of limiting beliefs about ourselves from childhood. In order to change, we must understand how our families, our cultures, and our media shape our perceptions of the world. By becoming conscious of the limiting beliefs and perceptions we have about what it means to be a man, we open the door to change. Awareness is the key! By becoming aware, we open ourselves up to the possibility to change and to break through our cultural conditioning.

When it comes to knowing thyself, I believe the most important thing a man can do is heal his heart and invest in his emotional well-being. Most Black men are not willing to discuss their emotions because our cultural conditioning says that we are supposed to be tough and non-emotional. We are terrified of being labeled as 'soft' or 'sissies' or 'punks', and we therefore refuse to examine our emotional lives. The fact of the matter is that we cannot be relational if we're unwilling to be emotional, and this is the primary reason so many of us have difficulty with our lives. We do not have the emotional tools to deal with the multiplicity of emotional and psychological challenges we face, so we resort to things like alcohol, drugs, sex, and work to try and deal with our unresolved pain.

To provide you with more insight on dealing with our emotions, I'd like to share an article I wrote, entitled "Men's Emotional Healing".

In 1989, I was experiencing a series of traumatic experiences that were beginning to take their toll. My divorce and separation from my kids were extremely painful and had begun to negatively impact my life. I had slipped into a deep state of depression and was barely able to function on a daily basis. As my depression deepened, I went into isolation, in which I literally shut myself off from the outside world.

Although I was able to go to work and function in that capacity, I was completely disconnected from any social settings. I was not dating. I did not socialize with my friends. I had difficulty sleeping. I would rarely eat, and I had began to lose weight, which was rare for me, being a former personal trainer that took excellent care of my physical body. After several months, I began to have fleeting thoughts of suicide, and it appeared that my situation was hopeless. In an effort to alleviate some of the pain, I began to read books dealing with depression.

As I read them, I could see myself in some of the stories. I definitely had all of the symptoms of depression, and I knew that I had to deal with it head on if I ever wanted to get my life back on track. After reading several books, I realized that I was still deeply depressed and had not really begun to deal with the issues that were causing my depression. Instinctively, I knew that I needed help, and I decided that I would go into therapy.

After making the decision to get help, another series of challenges surfaced. First of all, how was I going to find a therapist? How would I know which one to choose? What if the therapist couldn't help me? Would I be able to change? Could therapy "fix" me? What about the money? I was completely broke and definitely could not pay someone to listen to my problems. What was I going to do? These are just a few of the questions that were going through my mind.

My greatest fear was wondering what would happen if my employees found out. As a manager, I was considered the leader, and I definitely did not want to appear weak in front of my co-workers. I believed that I needed to keep this a secret so that I would not lose the respect of my employees.

In addition, I did not want my superiors to know because I thought I might lose my job if they found out.

After a few months of agonizing over these questions, I knew that I had to take the chance and try therapy. I didn't have any other choice. It was either seek help or die; there was no gray area. I decided that I definitely wanted to live, and I somehow gained the courage to go to a therapist office.

My first attempt at therapy did not go well. I walked into a therapist office and pretended that I was seeking information for a friend. I'm sure the people there knew this, but they allowed me to walk out with some of their brochures and a phone number to their suicide hotline.

To be honest, I was absolutely terrified. Although I was scared, deep down I knew that I would have to gain the courage to try again. I waited a few days and tried a different therapist office. This time, I had a completely different result.

As I walked into the office, I believe the receptionist picked up on my fear. I had begun asking her questions about depression and whether or not they had any books that I could read. All of a sudden, a therapist walked out and began asking me questions. "May I help you?" she asked. "Not really. I'm just looking for a little information about depression" "Are you depressed?" "I'm not really sure," I answered. "Why don't you come inside, and let's talk a little. Is that alright?" "I guess so."

As I followed her into her office, it felt as if my heart were going to jump out of my chest. I was so nervous and afraid that I was literally dripping with sweat. She obviously picked up on this and began to put my mind at ease.

"What is your name?"

"Michael."

"Well, Michael, I can sense that you are a little nervous, so let me start by asking what I can do to help you. Is there anything I can do for you?"

"Well, maybe. I have been doing some research about depression, and I think I'm depressed, but I'm really not sure."

"Do you feel depressed?"

"Based on what I've read so far, I think I am. But to be completely honest, I'm not sure I know exactly what depression is supposed to feel like. Does that make any sense to you?"

"It makes a lot of sense to me. Unfortunately, most men do not recognize how they feel. Men have been conditioned to disconnect from their emotions, and that makes it extremely difficult for men to express how they really feel. Most men will tell you what they think, but they usually do not know how they feel. You apparently fit into this category."

"I'm not sure if I really understand what you are saying, but a part of me thinks that you are right."

"You just validated the point I made. You are currently speaking from an intellectual perspective instead of an emotional one. It sounds as if you are disconnected from your emotions."

"Let's assume that you are right. If I am disconnected from my emotions, how do I get reconnected? Do you have any books on how to do this?"

"Unfortunately, you can not reconnect to your emotions by reading books. In order for you to reconnect, you have to relearn how to feel. This can be accomplished through therapy with me or any trained therapist."

"I really don't understand what you mean. But if I decide to relearn how to feel, how long will it take?

"I really can't answer that question. It's really up to you and how committed you are to doing the work."

"What do you mean, 'doing the work'? What kind of work is involved?"

"In the therapeutic community, we use the word 'work' because it takes a considerable amount of effort to heal yourself so that you can reconnect with your emotions. Doing the work means that you become willing to opening yourself up on an emotional level. This can be quite difficult at times."

"Well, I believe I'm ready. I'm really tired of being alone, and I definitely want to experience some fun in my life again. I think I can do this, so how much will it cost?"

"I operate on a sliding scale, based on your ability to pay. The most important thing is for you to make the commitment to yourself to heal, and we can address the money issue at a later date. Are you ready to begin? Let's set up a date and time for you to begin your healing."

"I just want to thank you for being so nice and understanding. The truth is, I was about to run out of your office before you showed up. Now, I am really glad that I came because I really believe that you can help me."

"That is a great attitude to have. I'm glad that you trust me enough to work with you. Just remember that I can guide you, but you must be willing to do the work. As long as you believe that you can heal, I can assure you that you will. Just stay committed and trust the process, and you will be just fine. The truth is, you have already done the hard part by showing up today. It takes an incredible amount of courage to be here, and I'm proud of you for taking the first step."

As I left the therapist's office that day, I knew that I had just taken the biggest step of my life. I did not know what to expect, but I knew that I was willing to do whatever it took to heal my emotions and relearn how to feel. I became committed to my own healing, and I can now say that I am emotionally healed and connected to my authentic self.

As the therapist mentioned, it was not easy, but it was definitely possible. It has been one of the most challenging, yet most fulfilling journeys of my life.

I cannot put into words the joy I feel on a regular basis as a result of doing my emotional work. My relationships now work, my creativity and sense of reverence are enhanced, my love of nature has been rekindled, and my professional life is rewarding and fulfilling. I took the road less traveled, and it has made all the difference in the world for me.

I wanted to share this story because there is such a negative stigma about men and therapy that I believe it's time for a new conversation. In this new conversation, men will recognize the importance of healing their emotions, and they will put forth the effort to do their healing work.

When we learn to support each other in our growth, we can remove the fear and stigma of being emotionally vulnerable, which will ultimately result in us being happier human beings. I personally believe that this is the most important work men can participate in, and we must begin supporting each other through this process.

If we will gain the courage to do this work, we will see a decline in domestic violence, child abuse, alcoholism, and random acts of violence. The time has come for a new conversation about our emotional healing.

Are you willing to join the conversation?

(Coach Michael Taylor)

If I had to sum up the most important work I have ever done in terms of knowing myself, it would have to be my emotional healing. What I learned through this process was that my childhood upbringing had a powerful impact on my life as an adult. All of the abuse I endured as a child had directly affected my self-esteem and self-worth, and it wasn't until I became willing to deal with that unresolved pain that I healed my heart and gained freedom from the pain. Once I removed the pain, I was able to create healthy relationships and dynamic health, and I became authentically happy with my life and am able to support others in doing the same.

In our current male culture, most men aren't willing to discuss these issues. If you are reading this right now, know that you are a very special person and that there is a reason for you to be doing so. If you have been struggling with your relationships, your health, your finances, or simply feeling like your life could be a lot more rewarding and fulfilling, there is a good chance that you might need to do some emotional work.

This means that it's time for you to "Know Thyself" and to become willing to do whatever it takes for you to live an extraordinary life. Rest assured that you have everything you need within yourself to do this; all it takes is a willingness and commitment to living your best life. You can definitely do this. I believe in you!

If you're truly ready to begin the process of knowing yourself, I'd like to make a few suggestions on things you can do.

First of all, I believe that it is absolutely imperative that you commit to reading books. Reading is exercise for your brain, and it is extremely important to give your brain plenty of exercise. It is also important that you read books to provide you with new information to support you in making better choices in your life. It's been said that if you keep doing what you've been doing, you'll keep getting what you've always gotten. Reading books and learning new things is a surefire way to make sure that you're getting something different to occur in your life.

The next thing to consider is participating in workshops and seminars. Being willing to interact with like-minded people and having their support will definitely expedite your transformational process. If you aren't comfortable being in groups of other people, there are plenty of online webinars and seminars that you can participate in on your computer in the comfort of your own home. Making a commitment to lifelong learning is a surefire way of Knowing Thyself.

I am also a huge fan of audio programs. You can listen to lectures and audiobooks from a variety of authors that can assist you with gaining a deeper understanding of yourself. You can listen on your cellphone or media player, or you can purchase CDs. There are literally thousands of personal development programs available to you. All you have to do is commit to Knowing Thyself, and I can assure you that resources will magically appear for you. Of course, it is your responsibility to take action, but once you make the commitment, the Universe will support you.

Below, you will find a few resources that may be exactly what you're looking for right now. Check them out and see if they resonate with you.

Good luck along your journey!

Websites
www.coachmichaeltaylor.com
www.mankindproject.org
www.landmarkeducation.com
www.blackmenrock.net
www.anewconversationwithmen.com

Books
John Bradshaw – Homecoming & Healing The Shame That Binds You
Charles Whitfield – Healing The Child Within

"I believe in God, but not as one thing, not as an old man in the sky. I believe that what people call God is something in all of us. I believe that what Jesus and Mohammed and Buddha and all the rest said was right. It's just that the translations have gone wrong."
John Lennon

Key #2: Develop A Spiritual Connection That Nurtures Your Soul

As a former atheist, it is somewhat of a miracle that I'm even writing this chapter. I remember a time in my life when just the mention of the word 'God' would turn me off and cause me to become defensive and close-minded. I had come to my own conclusion about God, and that conclusion was that God didn't exist. It was a point of view that I strongly held for several years, and during that time there was no way that you could convince me otherwise.

As fate would have it, I then had several "transcendent" experiences that changed my heart and mind about God. As a result of these experiences, and more than 15 years of research, I can now attest that I have developed a spiritual connection that nurtures my soul and is the driving force of my life.

My intention with this chapter is not to try and convince you that God exists or get you to join some organized religion. My intention is simply to challenge you to examine your beliefs and thoughts about God and possibly give you a different perspective about the divine.

I want to begin by sharing an excerpt from a study done by the Pew Research Center. It was entitled "A Religious Portrait Of African Americans", and it was published on January 30, 2009.

While the U.S. is generally considered a highly religious nation, African-Americans are markedly more religious on a variety of measures than the U.S. population as a whole, including level of affiliation with a religion, attendance at religious services, frequency of prayer, and religion's importance in life. Compared with other racial and ethnic groups, African-Americans are among the most likely to report a formal religious affiliation, with fully 87% of African-Americans describing themselves as belonging to one religious group or another, according to the U.S. Religious Landscape Survey, conducted in 2007 by the Pew Research Center's Forum on Religion & Public Life. Latinos also report affiliating with a religion at a similarly high rate of 85%; among the public overall, 83% are affiliated with a religion.

The Landscape Survey also finds that nearly eight in ten African-Americans (79%) say religion is very important in their lives, compared to 56% among all U.S. adults. In fact, even a large majority (72%) of African-Americans who are unaffiliated with any particular faith say religion plays at least a somewhat important role in their lives; nearly half (45%) of unaffiliated African-Americans say religion is very important in their lives, and roughly three times the percentage who says this are among the religiously unaffiliated population overall (16%). Indeed, on this measure, unaffiliated African-Americans more closely resemble the overall population of Catholics (56% say religion is very important) and mainline Protestants (52%).

Additionally, several measures illustrate the distinctiveness of the Black community when it comes to religious practices and beliefs. More than half of African-Americans (53%) report attending religious services at least once a week, more than three in four (76%) say they pray on at least a daily basis, and nearly nine in ten (88%) indicate they are absolutely certain that God exists. On each of these measures, African-Americans stand out as the most religiously committed racial or ethnic group in the nation. Even those African-Americans who are unaffiliated with any religious group pray nearly as often as the overall population of mainline Protestants (48% of unaffiliated African-Americans pray daily vs. 53% of all mainline Protestants), and unaffiliated African-Americans are about as likely to believe in God with absolute certainty (70%) as are mainline Protestants (73%) and Catholics (72%) overall.

So, what the report is saying in a nutshell is that Black people are the most religious people in the country, which leads me to the question I asked my grandfather when I was a little boy: "Why is God so angry at Black people?" If Black people are so religious and pledge their loyalty to God more than any other group, why do we have to endure so much injustice and pain? Why does it appear that God has turned His back on us?

My grandfather's answer was that God has a plan and that we should simply trust that plan. My answer now, as a result of my 15 years of research, is this: God is not the problem; our beliefs about God are the problem.

As the report mentions, Black people are the most religious people in the country. Collectively, we are an extremely religious group. My speculation is that we are probably religious as a result of all the atrocities and injustices inflicted on us as a group. Without our faith, I cannot see how we would have survived all of the challenges placed in front of us.

But now that we live in a different time - and without question, a different country - from what it was 100 years ago, isn't it time for God to begin showing us some love? Shouldn't we be reaping some blessings from above because of our loyalty to God and our faith? The answer lies in my previous comment: God is not the problem; our beliefs about God are the problem.

For the past fifteen years, I have been seeking to come to my own understanding about God. I have meditated with Buddhists, shared sweat lodge ceremonies with Native Americans, visited Jewish synagogues, prayed with Hindus, and engaged in dialogue with physicists. I am a member of a Christian church, although I really don't consider myself to be a Christian. I believe in Christianity as a way of life, and I try to the best of my ability to live a Christ-like life.

I have taken the time to come to my own understanding about God, and as I mentioned, I have created a spiritual connection that nurtures my soul.

I have read countless books dealing with God and spirituality, and each one of them has supported me in finding the answers I was seeking. But of all the books I have read, there is one series of books that has truly shaped my beliefs about God more than any other. It is a series of books entitled *Conversations With God*, by a gentleman named Neale Donald Walsch.

When I read his first book back in 1998, I literally couldn't put it down. Each word spoke directly to my heart and soul and confirmed for me what I had always believed about God: that God is literally unconditional love. God isn't some old white guy in the sky, taking notes about my life and waiting for me to screw up so He can banish me to hell. God is the infinite intelligence that created and is still creating this amazing Universe. God is not something to fear, but something to open my heart to because it is always there, just like my breath; all I have to do is come to the realization of this truth, and I can experience God in every moment and in every experience.

As I mentioned at the beginning of this chapter, I have had some transcendental experiences that have confirmed for me that God is real. Reading *Conversations With God* was one of those experiences. His writings literally changed and deepened my life.

My intention is not to try and convince you that God exists. I will, however, highly recommend that you consider reading Neale's books. They are deeply spiritual and contain what I consider to be divine truth.

I would like to share a very powerful teaching that I learned from Neale. It is called Five Steps To Peace, and when fully grasped, I believe it can transform your life in myriad ways. As I share the five steps, I will also share my own individual experiences of learning each step and how they helped me develop my spiritual connection.

Remember what I said: God is not the problem; our beliefs about God are the problem.

Here are The Five Steps To Peace:

Permit ourselves to acknowledge that some of our old beliefs about God and about Life are no longer working.
Explore the possibility that there is something we do not understand about God and about Life, the understanding of which could change everything.
Announce that we are willing for new understandings of God and Life to now be brought forth, understandings that could produce a new way of life on this planet.
Courageously examine these new understandings, and if they align with our personal inner truth and knowing, enlarge our belief system to include them.
Express our lives as a demonstration of our highest beliefs, rather than as a denial of them.

Excerpt from *The New Revelations: A Conversation with God* by Neale Donald Walsch
www.humanitysteam.org
http://www.nealedonaldwalsch.com

I would now like to share my thoughts about the steps and how I have used them in my own life.

1. Permit ourselves to acknowledge that some of our old beliefs about God and about Life are no longer working.

The reason I became an atheist was that the things I had learned in church simply seemed irrational to me. Although I had attempted to accept traditional religious teachings, there was a part of me that completely rejected the idea. There was a part of me that simply could not accept the idea that a loving God would banish people to eternal damnation because of their sins, and it made no sense to me that the bible was the only revelation from God.

So, I permitted myself to acknowledge that my old beliefs about God were not working, which led me to creating some new beliefs about God that I could honestly embrace and adhere to.

2. Explore the possibility that there is something we do not understand about God and about Life, the understanding of which could change everything.

By becoming open to the possibility that there was something I did not understand about God, I challenged myself to be completely honest about how I felt about God. As a result of being open, I then realized that the problems I was having weren't really about God; they were about my understanding of God.

The real problem was what I had learned through the Baptist teachings simply did not align with my core beliefs. Once I figured this out, I then decided to try a different religion. I stayed within the Christian religion for a while, and when I didn't find what I was looking for, I then decided to try something other than Christianity, and that is how my spiritual journey began. By being willing to increase my understanding about God, it opened the door to me eventually finding a spiritual home that nurtured my soul.

3. Announce that we are willing for new understandings of God and Life to now be brought forth, understandings that could produce a new way of life on this planet.

By surrounding myself with like-minded people, I then announced that I was willing to embrace some new beliefs and ideas about God. By sharing my newfound beliefs with others, I put together a spiritual support system that nurtured me and validated my beliefs. It also challenged me to continue my quest of deepening my relationship with the God of my understanding, and the quest continues to this very day.

4. Courageously examine these new understandings, and if they align with our personal inner truth and knowing, enlarge our belief system to include them.

It took an incredible amount of courage for me to leave the religion of my youth and begin the journey to find my own truth. During my fifteen-year journey, I was often confronted with being the only Black person in spiritual retreats, workshops, and even churches; but I intuitively knew that ultimately finding God had nothing to do with race, so I really didn't care. I was on a mission to find the

God of my understanding, and there was no one or no thing that was going to keep me from finding what I was looking for.

After several years of searching, I was introduced to Unity Church Of Christianity. It was and still is a progressive and practical teaching that truly aligns with my own inner truth. It is a positive approach to Christianity that empowers and supports me to be the best human being that I can be. Once I began studying their teachings, I knew that I had found a place to call home. I then fully embraced their philosophy, and it is the foundation of my faith and the source of the spiritual connection that nurtures my soul.

5. Express our lives as a demonstration of our highest beliefs, rather than as a denial of them.

I have come to the conclusion that if anyone wants to know what God they believe in, all they have to do is look at their lives. Results don't lie. If your life is filled with struggle, uncertainty, and fear, this means that you believe in a God that expresses those things. On the other hand, if your life is filled with unconditional love, abundance, and joy, then this is a reflection of your God.

Each day, I do my very best to let my actions be a reflection of my faith. As a result of my faith, I can honestly say that my current life is filled with joy, passion, and unconditional love. But like the story of Jesus, I, too, had to be crucified and then resurrected in my faith. I had to be willing to go through the wilderness of doubt and fear until I developed unwavering faith and trust.

One of my favorite spiritual sayings is this: "What I am is God's gift to me. What I make of myself is my gift to God." I am committed to becoming all that God created me to be, and by sharing my gifts of writing and speaking with the world, I am actually giving my gifts back to God.

So these are the 5 Steps To Peace:

1. Permit ourselves to acknowledge that some of our old beliefs about God and about Life are no longer working.

2. Explore the possibility that there is something we do not understand about God and about Life, the understanding of which could change everything.

3. Announce that we are willing for new understandings of God and Life to now be brought forth, understandings that could produce a new way of life on this planet.

4. Courageously examine these new understandings, and if they align with our personal inner truth and knowing, enlarge our belief system to include them.

5. Express our lives as a demonstration of our highest beliefs, rather than as a denial of them.

I'd like for you to take a moment and ask yourself a few questions:

Do you truly believe in God?
Is the God of your understanding an angry, judgmental, jealous God?
Do you see God as an anthropomorphic being that sits on a throne in Heaven?
Do you feel an intimate connection with God?

Too many people simply accept the beliefs about God that were passed down through their families and never really take the time to examine on a deep level what they believe about God. By following the five steps to peace, it could possibly open you up to some new beliefs about God that could change your life for the better.

Developing a spiritual connection that nurtures your soul is a very personal and private process that you must partake on your own. You must be willing to listen to your own inner guidance and find the path that is right for you. If you have questions or doubts about God, then it is your responsibility to answer them and remove any doubt. Rest assured that it is possible for you to develop a deep, intimate connection with a power greater than yourself that will bring you peace, comfort, and serenity, but you must be willing to let go of old, antiquated beliefs about God and embrace some new ways of being and relating to God.

I would like to close this chapter with my all-time favorite prayer. It is actually a poem that I converted into a prayer. This is the prayer I would read over and over again whenever I felt lost, lonely, or afraid. It carried me through some of the most difficult times in my life, and it was the beacon of light for me as I embarked on my spiritual journey.

The poem received a lot of attention in 1971 when it was taken to the moon by astronaut James B. Irwin on Apollo 15. Irwin's mother gave it to him before the flight, and he actually left a copy of the poem on the moon. The author, James Dillet Freeman, is Poet Laureate of the Unity School of Christianity at Unity Village. He wrote the poem in 1947.

I AM THERE

Do you need Me ?
I am there.
You cannot see Me, yet I am the light you see by.
You cannot hear Me, yet I speak through your voice.
You cannot feel Me, yet I am the power at work in your hands.
I am at work, though you do not understand My ways.
I am at work, though you do not understand My works.
I am not strange visions. I am not mysteries.
Only in absolute stillness, beyond self, can you know Me
as I AM, and then but as a feeling and a faith.
Yet I am here. Yet I hear. Yet I answer.
When you need ME, I am there.
Even if you deny Me, I am there.
Even when you feel most alone, I am there.
Even in your fears, I am there.
Even in your pain, I am there.
I am there when you pray and when you do not pray.
I am in you, and you are in Me.
Only in your mind can you feel separate from Me, for
only in your mind are the mists of "yours" and "mine".
Yet only with your mind can you know Me and experience Me.
Empty your heart of empty fears.
When you get yourself out of the way, I am

there.
You can of yourself do nothing, but I can do all.
And I AM in all.
Though you may not see the good, good is there, for
I am there. I am there because I have to be, because I AM.
Only in Me does the world have meaning; only out of Me does the world take form; only because of ME does the world go forward.
I am the law on which the movement of the stars and the growth of living cells are founded.
I am the love that is the law's fulfilling. I am assurance.
I am peace. I am oneness. I am the law that you can live by.
I am the love that you can cling to. I am your assurance.
I am your peace. I am ONE with you. I am.
Though you fail to find ME, I do not fail you.
Though your faith in Me is unsure, My faith in you never
wavers, because I know you, because I love you.
Beloved, I AM there.

James Dillet Freeman

*"Whether you believe you can or believe you can't,
you will always be right."*
Henry Ford

Key #3: Develop A Positive Mental Attitude

Since I was a child, I have always maintained a positive mental attitude. Somehow, I was blessed with the ability to always find the good in any situation, and I believe that is the primary reason I have been able to overcome a lot of my life's challenges.

But growing up in the 70's, my positive mental attitude was sometimes used against me. During the Civil Rights Movement, I firmly believed that being Black was a positive thing. Although I recognized the injustices inflicted on Black people, I still believed what my grandfather said about God never making a mistake, so I accepted what he said and always believed that I was the master of my own destiny.

But I remember arguments with friends in which I was called a sell out because of my attitude and beliefs. I remember being told that I truly didn't understand the "struggle" because I refused to blame white people. There were also times when I actually felt alienated from Black people simply because I was an optimist, and it sometimes caused me to feel isolated and alone.

Thankfully, my positive attitude and my beliefs that Black people would overcome the challenges of the 70's have been realized. As I look at all of the progress Black people have made in this country within my short lifetime, it solidifies my belief that the future is bright for Black people and the world at large.

Amazingly, there are still a lot of people who will completely disagree with my optimistic outlook. As a matter of fact, I believe most people would probably say that I'm too optimistic. They will point to things like the economy, civil unrest around the world, racism, and global warming as justifications of why I should be a little more pessimistic. From a Black male perspective, they will point to things like high incarceration rates, high school dropout rates, drug abuse, violence, poverty, and single parent homes to support the idea that Black men are an endangered species and a burden on society, and therefore I should be pessimistic about the future of Black men.

But I choose to view the world through an optimistic lens. I refuse to buy into the negative media generated perception that the world is a scary place filled with fear, anger, hatred, and greed. Although I recognize that these things exist in the world, I simply choose to focus my attention on what is right with the world versus what's wrong with it. From this point of view, I see people who are loving, compassionate, caring, and supportive. I see a world filled with unlimited possibilities for anyone who is willing to work hard and make their dreams come true. I see a world that is coming together, not falling apart, and as we enter into 2013, I am extremely optimistic about what the future holds.

So why do I remain so optimistic? It's actually pretty simple. It is a result of my attitude.
Thomas Jefferson said this: "Nothing can stop the man with the right mental attitude from achieving his goal; nothing on Earth can help the man with the wrong mental attitude."

Without question, attitude is everything. If you are committed to living an extraordinary life, then maintaining a positive mental attitude is paramount.

So if attitude is so important, why is it so difficult for most people to have positive ones?

The simple answer is that we are constantly bombarded with so many negative images through our media, our culture, and our families. They create negative beliefs in our subconscious minds, and all of these negative mental images end up becoming our attitudes.

The good news is that attitudes can be changed. No matter how negative your attitude might be, it is definitely possible for you to change it to be more positive.

The first thing you have to do is understand what your attitude really is. So, I would like to share my definition of attitude, then explain how you can change yours if you'd like.

Michael Taylor's definition of attitude is this: "The compilation and expression of your thoughts, feelings, and beliefs."

If a person has negative thoughts, feelings, and beliefs, he will usually act out in negative ways; therefore, we would say that he has a negative attitude. His actions are the results of his attitude, and therefore whatever is going on inside of a man will eventually show up outside of him as well.

A simple way to understand attitudes is to look at them as a series of beliefs and ideas that we hold in our subconscious mind. These beliefs begin at a very early age, and we usually aren't even aware that we have them.

For example, if you were raised in a family in which you constantly heard things like "Money is the root of all evil", "Money doesn't grow on trees", or "Rich people are greedy and selfish", then there is a good possibility that you have negative beliefs about money. If you do, then it will always be difficult for you to have lots of money because you have negative beliefs associated with money.

If you were raised in an environment where you were taught that white people couldn't be trusted, that racism would keep you from succeeding, and that life was going to be a struggle, then you probably have the subconscious belief that Black people can't succeed in this country. Until you change these internal beliefs, it will be difficult - if not impossible - for you to live an extraordinary life.

So, the way to change your attitude is to change your thoughts, feelings, and beliefs. This takes a considerable amount of effort, but I am absolutely convinced that anyone can change their attitude, and I will provide you with some ways to do this in a moment.

For the past several years, I have been researching men's issues, and I have come to the conclusion that as men, the time has come for us to change our attitudes and our beliefs about what it means to be a man. We must be willing to accept the fact that the old beliefs about what it means to be a man need to be replaced with some new beliefs that empower us to live more rewarding and fulfilling lives.

Here is an introduction from my previous book that really captures what I'm talking about. It's entitled "Why men are frustrated, tired, and hungry".

It is my fervent belief that men are frustrated, tired, and hungry. They are frustrated because they are trapped in an old paradigm that no longer works. They are frustrated because they are searching for new and better ways to exist as a man, yet they have failed in this search. They don't know where to turn, and they are becoming desperate for a new way of being and relating as a man.

They are tired of watching their families fall apart, their health deteriorate, and their wallets be emptied by divorce, materialism, and senseless addictions that rob them of not only their money, but their self esteem and dignity as well. They are tired of working at jobs that they hate just to try to keep up with the Joneses. They are tired of the emptiness and feeling of meaninglessness in their soul that tells them that there has to be another way to exist, yet they don't know how to change.

They are hungry for something new and different, and I believe that something different is A New Conversation with Men.

I know this because I used to be one of those men. I know what it's like to be frustrated, tired, and hungry, and for the last twenty years, I have been removing this frustration, eliminating my exhaustion, and satisfying my hunger to become a better man. As a result, I will admit that my life is now working, and I feel happy and blessed to be a man. I wanted to share my story in hopes of empowering you to follow in my footsteps. I simply want you to become a better man.

This book is written to assist any man who wants to do just that: become a better man. It is written for the man who is sick and tired of being sick and tired, and it is written for that courageous man who refuses to settle for mediocrity and wants to live a life of excellence.

It's been said that "There is no power in the universe that can stop an idea whose time has come." I believe the time has come for A New Conversation with Men, and there is nothing that can stop it. This book has been written to start a new revolution for the hearts, minds, and souls of men everywhere, and my hope is that this revolution changes the world for the better."

For the past six years, I have been hosting a radio show entitled "A New Conversation With Men" (www.blogtalkradio.com/ancwm) My intention has been to help men change their attitudes and beliefs about what it means to be a man. The show has supported men around the globe to embrace these new ideas about masculinity, and it has empowered literally thousands of men to change their attitudes for the better.

Here is another article that I wrote that I believe can help men change their attitudes about being a man. It's entitled "Men Are Not The Problem".

"With all of the negative publicity surrounding men, it's easy to see why men get such a bad rap in society. Turn on any news channel right now, and chances are you will see one of the following stories: senseless acts of violence, corporate corruption, divorce, DWI, pedophilia, infidelity, and the list goes on and on. So the question I pose is this: 'Are men the real problem?'

At first glance, it may appear that the answer is a resounding 'Yes'. Men do perpetuate a lot of the aforementioned social ills in society, and if we based our answer entirely on the media stories, then we could come to the conclusion that men are guilty as charged.

So once again, I pose the question: 'Are men the real problem?'

My contention is that the answer is an emphatic 'NO!'

It is my fervent belief that men are not the problem; the problem is that men are trapped in an antiquated paradigm of masculinity, which contributes to most negative male behavior. To clarify what I mean, I'll begin by giving you my definition of a paradigm. 'A paradigm is a rigid way of believing, thinking, and behaving.' You will not find this definition in a dictionary or other scholarly document. It is a definition that I created to help men understand how a lot of our behaviors are driven by unconscious societal programming. When we are able to grasp this definition, it opens the door for us to begin understanding why some men act the way they do, and it lays the foundation for us to create some concrete solutions to the challenges men face. This in no way excuses negative male behavior; every man is 100% responsible for his actions. By understanding the word 'paradigm', we can then get to the 'cause' of negative male behavior instead of only dealing with the effects of that behavior.

In the old paradigm of masculinity, men accepted that our roles were pretty simple. We were supposed to provide for and protect our families. Our job was to 'bring home the bacon' and 'discipline the kids'; therefore, most of us bought in to the American dream, which consisted of having the wife, the house, the 2.5 kids, and the 401K. Once we accomplished these things, we declare that 'we made it', and therefore our lives should be complete. In this paradigm, men are not taught about the importance of our own psychological, emotional, and spiritual well-being; therefore, we neglect our own needs for the needs of our family and others, and that is why our dreams sometimes turn into nightmares.

Speaking from experience, I was definitely trapped in the old paradigm back in 1989. I had done everything I thought I was supposed to do in order to be a man, yet my life was a mess. Within a six-year period, I went from having everything to having nothing. I went through a divorce, bankruptcy, foreclosure, and a deep state of depression, and it got to a point where I even considered suicide. I was trapped in the old paradigm of masculinity, and I had no idea how to get out. Fortunately for me, I heeded the advice of M. Scott Peck and took the road less traveled. I chose to begin my journey of transformation, and as a result I was able to break free from the old paradigm that I'm speaking about.

As a result of my twenty-year journey, I discovered that what I needed to do was first examine my deep rooted, long held beliefs about what it means to be a man. This took courage, discipline, and rigor, and I had to be willing to confront several erroneous beliefs about masculinity that were driving my behaviors, beliefs like that to be a man you must be non-emotional and disconnected, or to be a man you must have money and material possessions, and to be a man you must use sexual conquest as a gauge for manhood. These were just a few of the beliefs that I had to confront head on in order to break free. After discovering how my beliefs affect my thoughts, I then had to incorporate some new thoughts into my mind that supported my new understanding of masculinity. Thoughts like, 'It's OK to express my emotions openly and honestly', 'I don't have to have material possessions to be loved', and 'I can still be comfortable about my masculinity, even if I choose to be celibate.' These new ways of thinking, in turn, began affecting my actions. As a result, I began sharing my emotions openly and honestly. I was no longer afraid of being labeled 'weak' or overly sensitive, and I became authentic in expressing how I really felt, not just what I was thinking. As a result, all of my relationships became deeper and more intimate, and I was able to get out of my head and into my heart and truly connect with others. I then made the commitment to find my life partner, and I am happy to announce that I have been happily married for the past ten years and that I have a marriage that truly nurtures and supports me.

This is what the new paradigm of masculinity is all about. It's about encouraging men to embrace new ways of being men in this ever-changing world we live in. It's about making it OK for men to be emotionally vulnerable and connected and removing the fear that in doing so, they will not risk losing their masculinity. It's about breaking free from antiquated beliefs and behaviors that cause so much pain and suffering in our lives. It's about empowering men to become better husbands and fathers. It's about challenging men to create rewarding and fulfilling relationships and challenging men to create meaningful careers and dynamic health. In summary, it's about supporting men in becoming genuinely happy with their lives.

When society collectively recognizes that the old paradigm of masculinity no longer works, then makes a conscious choice to embrace a new paradigm, we will recognize that men are not the problem, but they definitely are the solution."

Ultimately, as men we must be willing to change our own attitudes. I hope these two articles will provide you with some food for thought to assist you in doing so.

I would now like to share 10 things you can do to develop a positive mental attitude. As I mentioned before, everyone can change their attitudes if they choose, but they must be willing to put forth some effort to do so.

Before I share the 10 keys, I want you to remember this quote: "If you keep doing what you've been doing, you will keep getting what you've always gotten." Be willing to do something different in your life if you truly want to change any aspect of it.

Here is the list of the 10 Things You Can Do To Develop A Positive Mental Attitude:

1. **Take complete responsibility for your attitude.**

    You must understand that you are 100% responsible for your attitude. Although the media may bombard you with negative images and your family may have exposed you to lots of negative influences, you and you alone are responsible for your attitude.

    Changing your attitude is an inside job, and it will require you to be willing to examine your beliefs and be willing to change them if needed. Taking responsibility for your attitude means that you refuse to remain a victim. It means that you choose not to place blame on anyone else and take complete responsibility for your thoughts, feelings, and beliefs. Everyone will be victimized in some way, but you get to choose whether or not you remain a victim. Choose not to be a victim! Take responsibility for your attitude!

2. **Limit Your Exposure To The Negative Media**

    It's been said that CNN stands for 'Constant Negative News.' This is true of most of our media. If you truly want to develop a positive mental attitude, you must stop filling your mind with so much negativity. From a Black male perspective, the images you will see throughout the media will usually be negative. Be sure to focus your attention on the positive stories, and don't believe the hype of our negative media.

3. Surround Yourself With Positive People

The people you hang around are a direct reflection of your beliefs. If you truly want to develop a positive mental attitude, make sure that those people are positive. This can be difficult at the beginning, but it is mandatory. You might have to change friends or associates, but rest assured it will pay off in the long run. Positive people will encourage you to engage in positive activities. They will also support and encourage you rather than attempt to bring you down.

4. Be Conscious Of The Words You Use

It's important to realize that the words we use are a reflection of our inner beliefs. If you are constantly speaking negatively about your circumstances or about life in general, it is the result of negative subconscious beliefs. If you find yourself using excessive profanity, there is a good chance that it is time to change your vocabulary. Words are a reflection of your thoughts, so you must change your inner beliefs if you want your words to change. Remember that "thoughts become things", so stay conscious of your thoughts and the words you use.

5. Read Positive Books

Reading is exercise for the brain, and it is important that you give your brain a workout on a regular basis. Reading can also help change your unconscious beliefs by replacing negative beliefs with positive ones, so it is an important part of your personal development. Be sure to read books that will provide motivation and inspiration and will provide you with insights to develop a positive mental attitude.

6. Let Go Of Any Negative Emotions

If you are holding on to any anger or resentment towards anyone, make it a point to let go of it. This process is called forgiveness, and it is an important part of developing a positive mental attitude. If you are filled with negative emotions, it's virtually impossible for you to have a positive mental attitude. This also means that you must learn to forgive yourself for anything that you may have done in the past and learn to love and accept yourself just the way you are.

7. Learn To Meditate

Meditation is an excellent way to learn to relax and become aware of what you are thinking. The purpose is not to make your mind go blank; the purpose is to simply make you aware of what you are thinking. If you will stick to a meditation practice, the benefits are immeasurable.

8. Start A Journal

Journaling is an excellent way to examine your hidden subconscious beliefs. It encourages self-reflection, helps clear your mind, improves mental health, releases pent up emotions, and helps in the healing process. It doesn't have to be perfect, and you don't have to worry about spelling. It is a commitment that you make to yourself and keep to yourself. It is a private process that you don't have to share with anyone, and if you commit to it, your journal can actually become a trusted companion.

9. Play & Laugh

Be sure to take some time each day to laugh and play. Laughter is a surefire way to improve your attitude. There are lots of things you can do to help yourself laugh and play. Watch a funny video, read a funny article, play with children, go play in nature, or listen to your favorite music. Make time each day to laugh and play, and I can assure you that it will support you in creating a positive attitude.

10. Develop An Attitude Of Gratitude

If you took 10 minutes a day and simply wrote down ten things you were grateful for, your attitude would change for the better in no time. When we focus our attention on what we are grateful for, we are blessed with more things to be grateful for. Keeping a gratitude journal and making a list of the things you are grateful for will warm your heart and help you focus on what is right with your life versus what is wrong with it. You don't necessarily have to write them down, but if you simply take some time to focus your attention on what you're grateful for once a day, then you will reap the rewards of an attitude of gratitude.

So, these are the ten things you can do to develop a

positive mental attitude. It takes commitment, persistence, perseverance, and faith to accomplish them, but you already have these qualities inside of you; now all you have to do is apply them to your life and make them happen.

Remember that the plan won't work if you don't work the plan, so work the plan and live an extraordinary life.

"The more connections you and your lover make, not just between your bodies, but between your minds, your hearts, and your souls, the more you will strengthen the fabric of your relationship, and the more real moments you will experience together."
Barbara de Angelis

Key #4: Make Relationships Top Priority

In 2008, when Barrack Obama first ran for president, I was inspired beyond words by his willingness to believe that he could become the president of the United States of America. I had never heard of him before this time, and to listen to him express his confidence that he could win ignited a fire within me that said, "If he can run for president in America, then anything is possible." I wasn't sure if he could win at the beginning, but the fact that he was smart enough and courageous enough to try empowered me. He immediately became a role model for me.

Now that he has won a second term, it reconfirms what I've always believed, which is if you have a dream and are willing to commit to that dream and put forth the effort to manifest it, in this country anything is possible. It does not matter what color you are, how old you are, what your educational background may be, or what social status you may come from. In America, if you can dream it, you can live it.

What impressed me as much as his willingness to run for president was his willingness to model what is possible for men in terms of relationships. There were many times that I watched him and Michelle together, and I became overwhelmed with pride to see him be such a loving, caring, sensitive, compassionate, involved husband and father. He single handedly showed the world that Black men are definitely capable of being all of these things, and he has dispelled a lot of the negative stereotypes about Black men and relationships.

I remember having this same feeling of pride when "The Cosby Show" first came out; but, unlike the fictitious Dr. Cliff Huxtable, President Obama is a real life example of what is possible for us as men who are committed to creating loving, supportive, monogamous relationships.

One thing that did surprise me was the response from the Black community about his relationship. It appeared to me that a lot of Black people were stunned and surprised to see a Black man be so affectionate and loving in public. It was as if the Black community viewed him as a Black male anomaly, as if they had never seen a Black man participate in relationships in this manner. I knew some white people would probably be a little shocked, based on the negative portrayal of Black men and relationships, but to hear Black people act so surprised that a Black man was capable of being such an amazing husband and father caught me off guard.

There was even a minor backlash from some Black men who said that now Black women would set their standards too high and expect all Black men to be like Barack.

The truth is, there are lots of Black men who are awesome husbands and fathers. We are not an anomaly. We are capable of being monogamous, supportive, intimate, and nurturing. We have these qualities within us; unfortunately, too many men are not willing to access them.

Creating loving family units must now become one of our top priorities. Healing the hurt and animosity between men and women is the foundation of the family. Right now, there are too many women who assert that they don't need a man, and there are way too men who claim that they don't ever want to get married. If we are serious about creating two-parent households, which are ideal for supporting our children in growing up emotionally and psychologically healthy, then we must begin by having a new conversation about relationships, then make a commitment to making relationships top priorities in our lives.

As men, a lot of us have not had direct access to men who are as open and loving as Barack Obama. Now that he has modeled such positive behavior, my hope is that more men will begin seeking out ways to become better husbands and fathers, just like our president. My attempt with this chapter is to share some insights I have gained in learning how to be a committed father and loving husband. The things I am about to share come from my own research and experience as a husband and father. I have also been heavily involved with men's work for more than fifteen years, and as the author of three books dealing with men's issues, rest assured that I can be considered an authority on this topic.

This does not mean that I am an expert; it simply means that I have invested a lot of time and energy in understanding male behavior, and the insights I've gained have allowed me to raise three amazing children (32, 29, & 26 years old) and to create a wonderful ten-year marriage that is both rewarding and fulfilling.

Before I share some insights on some specific things you can do to create healthy relationships, I want to share an article I wrote about a topic that a lot of men aren't comfortable speaking about. That topic is divorce. Divorce is one of the most difficult and painful experiences a man will ever go through. Too many times, we attempt to deal with this issue in isolation and fear. My intention with the article is to let men know that it is okay to talk about divorce, and more importantly to let men know that they can bounce back from divorce and eventually create a wonderful relationship or marriage if they choose to.

The article is entitled: "Bouncing Back From Divorce"

"I WANT A DIVORCE!" Although it's been over twenty-two years since I heard these words, I still remember the shock and uncertainty I felt when my former wife screamed them at me. Although I knew there were problems in our marriage, I really didn't believe that they were insurmountable. I knew that I was unhappy and felt trapped in a situation that I could not get out of, but now that I had a way out, I was unprepared to deal with it. I remember sitting up late that night and pondering what my next step should be. Should I go along with it and end our six-year marriage? What about the kids? Should I fight for custody? What will my friends and co-workers think? Where will I live? Should I give up the house? These were just a few of the questions running through my mind, and I had absolutely no idea how I was going to answer them.

The first few days after her divorce request were terrible. We would not speak to each other or even make direct eye contact. Although we continued to sleep in the same bed, we were emotionally miles apart from one another. We would simply go through our regular routines and walk past each other without saying a word. I could feel the tension between us, but I felt powerless to do anything. Every time I attempted to speak with her, our conversations would erupt into a shouting match. It appeared that there was nothing that could be done to save our marriage.

After several days, I was able to put my sadness and anger aside to try and make some rational decisions. I decided that it would be best if we at least attempted to save our marriage. There were several factors that prompted my decision. First of all, there were my children. As a child, I remember how much I missed not having a father in my life. I always envied my friends who had fathers, and I remember making a conscious decision to be a good father if I ever had children of my own. My children and I were very close, so I definitely wanted to minimize any pain they would experience. Another reason that I thought it would be best to stay together was financial. I knew that if we were to divorce, it would be extremely difficult for me to make it on my own while paying child support and possibly maintaining two households since my wife was a stay-at-home mom. Last but not least (and I'm not proud of this), I was really afraid of what my friends and employees would think of me. In their eyes, I had the perfect life. I had created this image of having it all together, and the thought of going through with this divorce would shatter that image. That really scared me and filled me with shame and embarrassment.

I convinced my wife to try marriage counseling. I told her that I really wanted to try and work things out, so we should at least give it a try. She agreed, and we began counseling. After several sessions, it became obvious that our marriage was not going to work out. I discovered that I really wanted out of the marriage, but I was too afraid to say it. All the reasons that I tried to make the marriage work were wrong. I never asked myself the two most important questions of my life: 1. Do I really love her? 2. Do I really want to spend the rest of my life with her? As a result of our counseling, I realized that the answer was "No" to both questions.

Once we knew that the divorce was inevitable, I decided to make it as amicable as possible. I sat down with her and said we should try to make this as simple and painless as possible. Fortunately, she agreed, and we were able to decide on how our possessions would be divided up. We were even able to work out visitation with the children. As a matter of fact, our divorce was so amicable that we used the same attorney to handle the divorce (if you are currently going through a divorce, my suggestion is that you do everything in your power to separate on good terms. Although this is extremely difficult, I can assure you that if you put your ego aside and try and work things out together, everybody wins in the end). I must admit that I am truly grateful to my ex-wife for being willing to work things out the way we did. I am forever indebted to her for never speaking badly to our children about me and for making sure that we worked together as parents to help our children handle the whole ordeal. Our willingness to work together to raise our children has paid off with three emotionally and psychologically well-adjusted children that we are both extremely proud of.

After the divorce was final, I found myself in unknown territory. This was actually the first time I had really failed at anything so major and life-changing. I did not know what to expect, but intuitively I knew that I would get through it. At the time, I was somewhat isolated and alone. I really did not have any close friends to talk to, so I simply kept to myself and tried to handle it alone. One of the first declarations I made was to never get married again. Marriage was a difficult and painful experience, and I concluded that I did not want to experience the pain and loss of a divorce ever again. To avoid the potential pain of relationships, I simply immersed myself in my work

After a few months, I decided to break out of my isolation and at least start going out again. Although I wasn't looking for a relationship, I did at least want to have some companionship. The problem I had with going out was that I was still ashamed and embarrassed because of my divorce, and I felt as if I had this huge neon letter 'D' stamped on my forehead. My feelings of inadequacy and failure made it extremely difficult to really connect with anyone, so most of the time I simply would go to clubs and dance a little without having much conversation.

Within approximately six months, I started to long for a relationship. I was tired of being alone, and I really missed having a partner to share life with. I decided to try and date to see what would happen. My first few relationships after my divorce were disasters. Although I did not know this at the time, I was absolutely terrified of intimacy. I had all sorts of trouble connecting on an emotional level with women because I was still scarred emotionally from my divorce. After several failures, I began to recognize a pattern in my relationships. The first thing I noticed was that my relationships never lasted more than three weeks. Within that time period, something would happen that would terminate the relationship. In most cases, the women were the ones who were saying that they weren't ready for a relationship. If they weren't leaving, I was the one making excuses about why I needed to end the relationship. I had devised some pretty good excuses for ending relationships, like being too busy at work or trying to be a good father to my children, but the truth was that I was terrified of experiencing the pain I had associated with relationships.

After a couple years, I met a woman that I really enjoyed being with. We had great chemistry and had a lot in common. After dating her for over a year, I began having deep feelings for her and decided that I really wanted to make a commitment to an exclusive relationship with her. When I told her how I felt, her response really caught me by surprise. She told me that she really liked me a lot and would like to develop a committed relationship with me, but she knew that I was emotionally unavailable to her, so she did not want to invest her feelings into a guy that could not reciprocate her love. I felt rejected and angry and did not know how to respond to her comment. As a result, the relationship ended, and there I was, alone again.

The good news is that I really listened to what she had to say. I recognized that I was the problem, not her. I was able to see that I was the reason my relationships weren't working out, and I decided to do something about it. I began my own inner journey to heal my heart so that I would no longer keep pushing women out of my life. I followed M. Scott Peck's advice and took the road less traveled, and I definitely became a better man as a result of it.

After being on my fifteen-year personal journey and learning to love myself, I decided that I really did want to remarry. Since I took the time to understand the how's and the why's of my past relationship failures, I was able to finally create loving and supportive relationships without the fear of intimacy or abandonment. As a result of my commitment to my own personal growth, I was able to create a relationship that really works for me, which ultimately resulted in me getting remarried and creating a marriage that really nurtures and supports me. I really enjoy the emotional security that comes from having a spouse that loves and adores me, and I'm truly grateful that I took the time to understand the importance of having authentic relationships.

Great relationships take effort and commitment, but ultimately they are definitely life's greatest treasure. If you are having difficulty with relationships, been through or are going through a divorce, or have a deep fear of

commitment, take the time to heal your heart, and it will open the door to creating great relationships.
Good luck!

So now I would like to share the 10 keys to creating healthy relationships. I can assure you that if you apply these keys to your life, you will create rewarding, fulfilling, and intimately connected relationships.

Number 1:

Develop a healthy relationship with yourself. For most men, I can assure you it is very uncomfortable for them to say, "I love myself." Why? Because for some people that may sound a little arrogant, a little cocky, a little narcissistic. The truth is, if you don't love yourself, you cannot love another person. It's not possible because all relationships begin with you. The first thing you have to be willing to do is create a healthy relationship with yourself. When you look in the mirror, ask yourself what do you see? Do you see someone that's trustworthy? Do you see someone that's lovable? Do you see someone that's dependable? Do you see someone in that mirror that you would want to be in a relationship with? Ask yourself that question honestly because that's where relationships begin.
They begin with you. If you want to create healthy relationships, start with yourself. Sometimes that means we have to take a break from relationships with other people and spend some time developing a relationship with ourselves. This may be uncomfortable or seem a little weird, but rest assured, it is the first thing you must do. Too many times, we want to point our fingers at the women in our lives, but the fact remains that if we want to create healthy relationships, it always begins with the man in the

mirror. We must take complete responsibility for our relationships and not blame anyone else except ourselves. Once we do this, we lay the foundation for great relationships.

<u>Number 2:</u>

Make relationships top priority. In our culture and in our society, a man's job has basically been two things: protect and provide. This has been true since the beginning of time. Think about it. What was a caveman's primary responsibility? He was supposed to find a cave to keep his little cavewoman happy and warm, and then he had to go out there to find food and make sure that he kept the dinosaurs from eating his family. Provide and protect.

Unfortunately, too many men are still trying to do that. They believe that if they just do these two things, then they will be happy. What we really need to do if we're going to make relationships top priority is to connect; not just provide and protect, but connect. Connection takes emotions, and too many times men do not have the emotional awareness to connect, which is a major cause of relationship failure.

What we usually do is focus all of our attention on our jobs, our bills, our cars, our stuff, and our kids, but we aren't doing anything to connect in our relationships. We aren't doing anything to deepen our connection.

The sad part is that a lot of men will go through life and work at a career, raise their kids, and do everything they can to try and keep up with the Joneses. Then they get close to retirement and start asking themselves, "What am I going to do?"

As soon as they retire and they're at home with their wives on a full-time basis, it's total chaos because now they have to connect with their spouse, but they don't know how to do that.

If they would have only made relationships top priority in their lives from the beginning, it would have made their lives a lot easier in the long run. Be sure to make relationships top priority in your life, and you, too, will be happier in the long run.

Number 3:

Relinquish the need to be right. That's it! Let go of the need to be right! It's sad, but most men would rather be right than happy. What happens is they get attached to being right, which creates disconnection, and then they wonder why they're so unhappy.

Did you know that in healthy, connected relationships, two people never have to fight? What do you mean, Michael? A relationship without fighting? That's not possible! Yes, it is! I can promise you that it is possible, and here's how: you must make the distinction between fighting and conflict. They aren't the same thing. Fighting is about being right. It's about being more concerned with being right than being happy.

On the other hand, conflict is what occurs when you bring two human beings together who will always have different opinions and beliefs. There's no way that you can avoid conflict in a relationship, but you can let go of your need to be right about the conflict, which will transform your relationships in an instant.

How many times have you had a fight over something really simple, and all you had to do was say, "That's okay," and let it go? But then there was a part of you that took this firm stand that you were just not going to let her be right. We've all done it. It's part of human nature to want to be right. Guess what? It doesn't work in relationships. Relinquishing your need to be right will transform your relationships in an instant if you will just be willing to let things go.

At the same time, there will be some things that you feel very strongly about, and you will choose not to compromise. You can do that without being attached to being right. You don't have to compromise your values in what's really important to you; you just have to be willing to say, "I don't have to be right. I'd rather be happy than right." When you do that, your relationships will transform immediately.

Number 4:

Be attentive to your partner. Being attentive to your partner means being in the present moment, fully aware of what they're saying, doing, and feeling. When we do that, we create connection. When you really pay attention to your partner and you're really concerned about what they're saying, connection is created. If you really want to create healthy relationships, you must be attentive to your partner; again, it creates connection.

Number 5:

Express affection to your partner. That doesn't mean that you have to go out in the street and kiss your wife in front of a lot of people. Affection means that you're in some way affirming that you care about her by touching and acknowledging and possibly kissing her. Affection doesn't necessarily mean kissing; you can just touch someone and show affection. The key is to be comfortable making physical contact with your partner. Touching is a way to create physical connection. Studies have shown that infants that are held and nurtured and physically touched are healthier than babies that aren't. It's in our DNA to be touched and held. Expressing affection shouldn't be a big issue unless you're stuck in your male ego, so let that go. Express affection to your partner.

Number 6:

Say I love you and mean it. If you truly love someone, why should it be difficult to tell them? When you say, "I love you." be sure to say it from your heart, not your head. Say it often, and mean it every time. If you don't feel it, don't say it.

Number 7:

Spend quality time with our partner. You have to define quality time, but quality time means you move away from all the hustle and bustle of life, the kids, the jobs, the house, and all of that, and you spend time where you're just hanging out. For some, it may mean just sitting on the back porch. For others, it may be going to a spa all day. You have to decide what it is, but it's important that you spend quality time where you're being attentive, where you're connecting with your partner. It's extremely, extremely important.

Number 8:

Loosen up, let go, have some fun. When was the last time you laughed with your partner? Just had a good laugh? If nothing comes to mind, something's wrong because relationships should be about fun, not just about stress and all the day-to-day challenges that we deal with. If you want to create connection, you have to have fun because whether we realize it or not, we all have this playfulness inside of us. It's there. Too many of us have pushed it down so far, we've forgotten what it feels like, but we have to bring that playfulness back up and have fun and recognize that it doesn't make you less of a man to do so.

Number 9:

Celebrate your victories together. Life is tough enough as it is. Just look around you. We have all these things going on in the world. Our one refuge should be our relationship and our homes. When you accomplish something or something positive happens in your relationship, you should celebrate that. It can be something as small as a hug or something as elaborate as taking your wife out to a really fine dinner because she got a promotion at work. The key is to recognize that you're in this together and you should be grateful that you have each other. When you overcome hurdles, that deepens your connection. Have some fun, celebrate your victories together, and acknowledge each other for being there for one another.

Number 10:

Count your blessings, not your problems. Too many times, we focus all of our attention on what's wrong versus what's right with our relationships. When you focus all of your attention on what's wrong, guess what happens? Disconnection. If you're in a relationship, it may not be perfect, but you know this person is there for you, and that's something to be grateful for. Count your blessings for what she does right. An attitude of gratitude goes a long,

long way in deepening your connection in relationships. Make sure that you're counting your blessings, not your problems. When you do that, I can assure you that connection happens and relationships bloom. That's just the way that it works.

There they are, The 10 Keys To Creating Healthy Relationships.

I realize some of you out there are going, "OK, Michael, you've just shared 10 keys to creating healthy relationships. I got it, but what I didn't get, what I didn't see, what I didn't hear you say, Michael, is anything about the sex? What about the sex, Michael? You didn't talk about the sex."

Here's a promise that I can make. It's actually a guarantee. I can absolutely, 100% guarantee that if you follow these 10 keys, if you create the connection that I'm talking about in relationships, there is absolutely no way, *no way* that you won't have great sex.

Here's why: too many times, we think that sex is about the physical act; in reality, making love is about the emotional and spiritual act. When you have your emotions involved and you have a deep connection with your mate, making love is deeper, more intimate, and more awesome.

Because when you really care about somebody, it's no longer just about physical sex. It's about sharing something, sharing a part of you. This whole process of connection is about moving past just having sex and making love. It doesn't mean you can't have some wild, crazy, passionate, physical love or sex. That could happen, too. What I'm saying here is that, as men, we put so much focus on the physical aspect of sex that we miss out on the emotional and spiritual connection; when you do that, you cannot have great sex. If you have trust, commitment, honesty, openness, all those things in your relationships, your sex life, your love life will work. I can guarantee you that. The question is, are you willing to accept it?

The question you're probably asking is, "Do these keys really work?" I know they do. How do I know? Because they work for me. If they work for me, they can work for you.

More importantly, I can honestly say that I have this type of connection with my wife. I have a marriage that works because I took the time to learn about me, I took the time to go through my emotional transformational process, and now it has allowed me to create this type of relationship. If I can do it, you can do it, too.

I want to close this chapter with a story. This story is called "The Nine-Cow Woman". It goes like this:

Once upon a time, there were these two friends that loved to sail and had this beautiful ship that they sailed around the world. One day, one of the guys decided that he was tired of sailing, and he wanted to settle down and get married.

So they go to this island, and the guy says, "I'm going to find the woman of my dreams on this island." His friend wishes him luck, and they begin walking around the island to find the woman of his dreams. As he is walking around the island, he looks across the street and sees this woman that he immediately falls in love with.

He points to his friend and says, "There she is. There's the woman of my dreams." His friend looks at the woman and says, "Excuse me? Not that woman standing across the street - because she's not that attractive."

"No, that's her. She's the one."

"OK. I trust you, I wish you good luck, but I am going to continue sailing."

His friend gets on the boat and leaves the island. The other guy stays on the island. He gets a chance to meet the girl, they go out, they fall in love, and he decides that he wants to marry her. On this island, there was a tradition, which was that before you married someone, you had to go to the father and pledge a certain amount of cows in exchange for the daughter's hand in marriage.

On this island, royalty received nine cows, while the average woman received three or four cows. And so the guy goes up to the girl's father and tells him that he has fallen in love with his daughter and would like to ask for her hand in marriage.

When the father asks him how many cows he would like to give for his daughter, the guy says he would like to give him nine cows. The father looked a little surprised and initially rejected the offer because he didn't think his daughter was worth the nine cows, but the guy refused to give him anything less than the nine cows because that was what he felt the woman was worth.

The father agreed, and the couple was married.

A few years pass, and his sailing buddy decides he wants to visit his friend. He comes back to the island, docks his boat, and begins walking through town. As he's walking through town, he notices a beautiful parade, and he also notices that there are a lot of beautiful women in the parade and on the island. For a brief moment, he even considers finding a woman for himself and settling down.

As he walks through town, he notices the most beautiful woman he's ever seen being carried through town. He admires her beauty for a moment, then continues to find his friend.

After a few moments, he finds his friend, and they embrace and begin to catch up on old times. His friend tells him that he met and married the woman of his dreams and that he was very happy with his life.

His friend then tells him about the beautiful woman he had seen in the parade, and he tells his friend about all of the other beautiful women he had seen on the island.

As they are sitting there on the porch, all of a sudden the beautiful woman he saw in the parade walks up to them and says hello. She then walks over to the guy who had stayed on the island and gives him a kiss.

The other friend looks at the woman, then looks at his friend and asks, "Who is this?" To which the friend replied, "This is my wife." "But that isn't the same woman you pointed out the last time I was here." "Yes, it is," he replied. "It can't be! The other woman was not this beautiful."

Then the woman looked at him and said, "I'm the same woman you saw, and I'm sure I look different. If you're wondering what happened to me, it's really pretty simple. All of my life, people have been treating me as though I were a 3-cow woman. Even my own father saw me that way. But my husband saw me as a nine-cow woman, and I simply chose to become the nine-cow woman that he knew I was."

The moral of that story is, too many times we see people in our lives as one-cow, two-cow, or three-cow people. The truth is, we're all nine-cow people; unfortunately, too many of us have forgotten that we are. Make a commitment to treat everyone as nine-cows, and I can assure you they'll become the nine-cow people that we see them as.

God bless you.

*"Never doubt that a small group of thoughtful, committed
citizens can change the world;
indeed, it's the only thing that ever has."
Margaret Mead*

Key #5: Develop A Positive Support Network

In 1995, I read a book that would literally change my perception about being a human being. The book was entitled *The Seat Of The Soul* by Gary Zukav, and it was an eye-opening experience that stretched the boundaries of my thinking about who I am as a man.

The premise of the book is that we are much more than just these limited physical bodies. He theorized that we are actually spiritual beings having a human experience instead of a human beings having a spiritual experience.

After reading the book, I knew that I wanted to continue learning from this amazing teacher. I began following him through television appearances and the Internet, and his teachings really helped me gain a deeper understanding of myself and this amazing Universe we live in.

After following his teachings for a couple years, he then introduced a way for me to deepen my learning and fully embrace some of his ideas. He introduced the concept of a Soul Circle, in which people joined small groups around the world to talk about his teachings and gain their own personal power.

After learning about these groups, I decided that I wanted to participate in one; unfortunately, there weren't any groups in my immediate area. I was so committed to participating that I decided I would start my own group.

I posted a flyer at my church and invited people to join. Within a couple days, a woman contacted me (I'll call her Julie) and said that she was interested. We decided to meet for lunch to discuss the creation of our Soul Circle.

At our first meeting, we shared our vision for building the circle. She was just as passionate and excited as I was to begin, but we really didn't have a structure to set it up. I had read some information on his website about the logistics of setting up the circle, but some of the things he suggested didn't feel right. So, she and I came up with our own format and laid the foundation for building our own circle.

Within approximately three weeks, we had ten members, and we would meet every Monday at Julie's house.

Participating in the Soul Circle was a new experience for me. I had always been a little uncomfortable in groups, so it took a lot of courage for me to be there. To be completely honest, I was absolutely terrified at the beginning, but I intuitively knew I needed to work through those fears. I knew that if I were truly committed to my growth, this would be the perfect place for me to be.

To give you, the reader, a better understanding of the intention of a Soul Circle, I wanted to share a description of a Soul Circle that I found online. It really captures the essence of what Soul Circles are all about.

INTENTION OF SOUL CIRCLES

1. **Accelerate Spiritual Growth:** Many of us are feeling the inner tug that now is the time to really step up our spiritual growth. The main purpose of the Soul Circles is to provide the tools, support, and environment for those seeking spiritual growth who are ready and willing to make the required effort.

2. **Support:** Spiritual growth is usually not easy since it requires us to make changes to our habitual behavior. It is only by making positive changes in our thoughts, words, and actions that real progress happens. The Soul Circles will provide a safe, loving, and non judgmental environment to share our progress and our struggles on our individual and unique paths.

3. **Empowerment:** As we grow our intuition and learn to trust it, we will be guided by our higher Self to step out of our comfort zones and stretch ourselves to more fully realize our true purpose here. It is only through our spiritual work that we can be empowered to fully realize our potential and play our part in creating a world of peace and harmony. To further build our empowerment, each member, on a rotating basis, will facilitate the meetings.

4. **Knowledge of Spiritual Truths:** We will research, study, and share the many spiritual truths and universal principles that govern how things operate on our planet and beyond. For example, how the Law of Attraction works to manifest what we put our attention on. The knowledge of the spiritual truths provides the foundation for changing the world and building our own paths to mastery.

5. **Harmony with Spiritual Truths:** Through self-examination, we will become aware of areas in our life that are not in harmony with these spiritual truths and how they are not serving us. Then, we will explore ways to be in harmony with these Truths by making the necessary changes in our lives in order to raise our consciousness.

6. **Service:** When we serve others, the obvious benefit is to those that it helps and heals, and as we know, there are many in need; but just as importantly, when we give

unconditionally from a place of love, we get so much more back in return in the way of love and soul growth.

7. **Live Soul's Purpose:** Each of us has a blueprint of our spiritual plan for this lifetime and the lessons that our soul has chosen to learn. The deep work done in the circles will help shed light on this so that we can better live our soul's purpose.

Participating in the Soul Circle transformed my life. In the circle, I was able to speak openly and honestly about anything. It challenged me to take a really deep look at my insecurities and fears, as well as my hopes and dreams. In the circle, there is unconditional love and acceptance, and it provides a safe space to share anything without fear of judgment, criticism, or rejection. It is a place of growth and transformation, and I feel deeply honored to have been a part of such a learning environment.

I have been participating in a Soul Circle for approximately 13 years now. Although we only meet a couple times a year, the members of the circle are some of my closest friends. They challenge me, support me, love me, and hold me accountable for being the best me that I can possibly be. I have been truly blessed by belonging to my Soul Circle.

I needed to share that story of my Soul Circle because if you are truly committed to living an extraordinary life, you must be willing to develop a positive support network. I realize that for most men, the three most difficult words for us to say is, "I need help"; therefore, most men are reluctant to participate in any type of group, but rest assured that your participation is mandatory if you truly want to grow and become the best you possible.

It is my belief that too many men live lives of isolation and desperation. Speaking from experience, I remember when I was married the first time and it appeared that everything in my life was perfect; the truth was, I usually felt alone and unhappy. Although I had all the things society says I was supposed to have, my life felt empty and meaningless. I then made the commitment to change my life, and putting together a positive support network really helped me accomplish that goal.

Here are 5 reasons why it's important for you to develop a positive support network.

1. **Everyone needs support**

This is probably the greatest lesson I've learned while participating in my Soul Circle. I have always struggled with asking friends for support. One of the reasons I had such difficulty with this issue is that I really found it difficult to trust people. By learning to trust my friends and myself, I've learned to be able to accept support and not try to carry the weight of the world on my shoulders alone. No man is an island, and everyone needs support at times.

2. **It gives you a different perspective of yourself.**

Have you ever wondered why all star athletes need coaches? It's because the coach can watch them from a different perspective and give them insights on how they can improve. The athletes have all of the talent, but the coach helps them enhance their talents from a different perspective. You already have all the talent you need within you; a positive support network can help you bring it out.

3. **A positive support network helps you make positive**

choices.

Have you ever seen a story in which an athlete gets in trouble because he continues to hang out with the wrong people? Although they may have access to lots of money and appear to have everything a person needs to be happy, they sometimes self-destruct because they are hanging around negative people. It can be difficult to let go of friends whom you may have grown up with, but if you're friends aren't a part of a positive support network, are they truly your friends? True friends are positive influences who should support you in making positive choices. If you make sure you surround yourself with a positive support network, chances are you will make positive choices in your own life.

4. Positive support networks can provide excellent networking opportunities.

When you have a positive support network, it can definitely open the door for other opportunities. As a result of participating in my Soul Circle, my friends supported me in myriad ways. I have received speaking engagements, CPA services, financial support, and even blind dates as a result of my positive network. The most important thing to remember is a quote from Oprah Winfrey: "Only surround yourself with people who will take you higher."

5. Positive support networks are the perfect opportunity to speak from your heart.

If you surround yourself with people who are committed to their own personal growth and will support you in yours, then you have the perfect place to learn to speak from your heart. Speaking from your heart means you learn to get out of your head and talk openly about your feelings. This is definitely difficult for most men, but it is the key to living a rewarding and fulfilling life.

I can fully understand why men are so afraid of participating in any type of support group. I remember how terrified I felt when I first began. Men find it extremely difficult and uncomfortable to experience vulnerability and intimacy, but this is what all men really need. Finding a positive support network is extremely important if you are truly committed to change. A great place to start might be your local church. If you aren't comfortable going to church, there are men's groups around the country that can provide you with the type of support that will help facilitate your transformation.

If you're not sure where to start and you're considering joining a group, here is a great resource for you. It is an organization called the Mankind Project, and it is one of the most empowering organizations for men in the country. I am a graduate of their New Warrior Training, and I highly endorse their work. You can find them online at: www.mankindproject.org. Once you get there, take a moment and read some of their testimonials, peruse their website, and click on the link that says 'Men's Groups". There will be lots of resources there to support you in getting in touch with a group, or they can even help you start your own.

If you have been struggling with drugs and alcohol, then Alcoholics Anonymous is an excellent resource to support you in dealing with addictions and recovery. It can be a powerful support network for you, and it can support you in rebuilding your life as you deal with your life's challenges.
The most important thing is for you to gain the courage to develop a positive support network, then make the commitment to stick with it. Good luck!

"The Matrix is a system, Neo. That system is our enemy. But when you're inside, you look around, what do you see? Businessmen, teachers, lawyers, carpenters. The very minds of the people we are trying to save. But until we do, these people are still a part of that system, and that makes them our enemy. You have to understand, most of these people are not ready to be unplugged.
And many of them are so inert, so hopelessly dependent on the system that they will fight to protect it."
Morpheus
from the movie "The Matrix"

Key #6: Do Not Buy In To The Negative Media

Several years ago, I was sitting in a restaurant when I overheard a conversation between two apparently well educated and well dressed young Black men. In the conversation, they were discussing the state of Black men in America, and they were saying that they did not believe that Black men would be around in twenty years. They honestly believed that Black men were going to become extinct.

Their rationale was obviously based on the negative media-projected stereotypes that most Black men were either going to be dead or in prison, and they obviously had accepted these stereotypes as true. They were definitely pessimistic about the future for Black men, and there was nothing I could have said to them that would have made them change their minds.

As a result of hearing that conversation, I decided that I needed to try and do something to change the minds of Black men. I recognized that this conversation was just a microcosm of how too many Black men felt, and I wanted to interject a different more positive perspective on being a Black man in America. So, I decided to write a book in hopes of sharing some insights in supporting them in succeeding.

In 1995, I wrote and published *Brothers Are You Listening? A Success Guide For The 90's*. It was a book that was targeted specifically to Black men in hopes of providing them with some tools to help them succeed, based on my own experience of overcoming some seemingly insurmountable obstacles in my own life.

When I began marketing the book and doing radio interviews, I was completely caught off guard by some of the negative attacks and criticisms of me and my book. Although most people seemed to agree with what I was attempting to do, there were some men who actually attacked me and accused me of being out of touch with being Black, simply because I believed that the media's depictions of Black men were inaccurate. I remember one specific caller who said that he also believed that Black men were in danger of becoming extinct and for me to say that Black men could succeed in America was ridiculous. He believed that no matter what Black men did, somehow this country was going to keep them from succeeding.

It's been approximately 17 years since I wrote that book, and without question a lot has changed for the better in this country since then. I still remain extremely optimistic about the future of Black men, while there are still some people who believe that Black men are an endangered species.

My intention with this book is to refute that claim.

Before I share my reasons for optimism and why I do not believe Black men are an endangered species, I wanted to share an article I wrote a while back, which I believe will set the context for this chapter.

It's entitled "The Trials And Triumphs Of A Joyful Black Man In America".

Growing up as a young Black male in the inner-city projects of Corpus Christi, Texas, I was acutely aware that being "Black" somehow made me different. As I watched television and looked through magazines and books, I realized that the people I perceived to have all of the wealth were white people. When I asked my mom the reason for this, her response was that there were lots of Blacks that were wealthy, but the white people did not want to show that on television. When asked why not, she responded by saying that this was the way that white people could control the minds of Black people and keep them from attaining wealth. Even as a child, there was something about that comment that I did not agree with. I wanted to understand how the mind worked, and most of all I wanted to understand how white people could control the minds of Black people.

As I progressed through elementary school, I remember the tension and fear I felt as I interacted with white kids in my class. At the age of nine, I had my first experience of racism when a white female classmate approached me after a spelling test. In this class, the person who scored an 'A' on a test would receive a gold star, which was then placed on a poster board in plain view for all the students to see. It just so happened that I had the most gold stars of anyone in the class, and the teacher would always encourage me to do well and be comfortable being at the top of the class, intellectually and academically. After this particular test, the white female classmate came up to me and said, "My mom says that all niggers are dumb and stupid, and even though you may have more stars than I do, I am still smarter than you." I stood there in shock and disbelief and was unable to respond. Even though I had the evidence to refute her comments, as a nine-year-old, the pain of her words cut me like a knife. I felt angry, yet ashamed because this was not the first time I had heard those words. But this was the first time that I had heard them targeted directly at me by one of my peers.

My most painful experience of blatant racism occurred when I was seventeen. I was in high school, and I met and fell in love with my high school sweetheart. She was a wonderful, supportive, caring person that incidentally happened to be white. When we met, she was somewhat of a wild child. She came from a pretty wealthy family, yet she hated her father and was into drugs and rebellion. She was a C and D student that liked to skip school and hang out at the beach with her friends. After going out with her for a while, I convinced her to turn her life around and give up the skipping school and abusing drugs.

She changed her attitude and became an A and B student. We were extremely close and shared that high school, infatuated kind of love that feels so deep that it stays with you for a lifetime. After going out with her for over a year, her father found out that we were dating. One night I got a phone call from him, and it was obvious that he was not happy.

As he began speaking, I knew that I needed to keep my cool and not disrespect him. I listened to his objections and gave him an opportunity to get everything off his chest. When he finished, I made the mistake of telling him that he did not have the right to decide whom his daughter should date. I tried to convince him that I had been a good influence on his daughter and that he should be happy that she was doing so well. My hope was that I could get him to understand that I was a good guy that was actually good for his daughter. Of course, he could not hear a word I was saying. He was adamant about the fact that he knew what was best for his daughter and that I was just some young punk trying to take advantage of his little girl. After screaming his disapproval of our relationship for several minutes, he then said something that completely caught me off guard. Although I knew he was angry, I did not expect to hear these words: "There is no way that I will allow my daughter to date a nigger. I will kill you before I let that happen." Although the words were painful, it was the venomous feeling of anger and hatred that came through the phone that ripped out my heart. Even today, almost thirty years later, I can still feel the hatred in his words. His anger came from deep within his soul, and it was apparent that his anger wasn't just about me, but about all Black people.

As I sat there in disbelief, I immediately went numb. A part of me wanted to defend myself and curse at him and retaliate in some way. My initial feeling was anger, which I quickly subdued to avoid getting into a shouting match. Another part of me was extremely afraid because I did not know whether or not he would actually attempt to take my life. But the feeling I remember most after his comment was sadness. I remember a sinking feeling in my gut that was the result of being invalidated as a human being. I knew that he viewed me as less than a man and in his mind I was not good enough for his daughter, simply because I was Black. It was dehumanizing and demoralizing. How could this man hate me so much and not know anything about me? How could he pass judgment on me without ever seeing me or speaking to me? Why could he not see the positive influence I had had on his daughter? Why was I not allowed the opportunity to meet with him and talk to him so that he could see how much I really cared about his daughter and that my intentions were to simply love and support her? So many questions, so few answers.

◆◇◆

I share these three true personal stories because as a Black man, I realize that my experiences are really just a microcosm of the challenges facing Black men, even today. I personally believe that our media still does an irresponsible job of portraying Black people in general. The media generated perception is that being Black is synonymous with being poor, uneducated, unmotivated, and somehow a burden on society. Although I do not believe that the media can control how Black people think, I am aware of the power that the media does have on a person's perception. Since a person's perception is their reality, the media definitely has an influence on people's minds.

It is my fervent belief that people in general are not born racist. Hatred is not a part of a person's genetic make up. Racism is something that is learned, and people usually learn from the environments in which they are raised. Unfortunately, there are still some parents that teach their children that Black people are inferior as human beings, and sadly enough, some Black people have accepted this as true.

As a Black man, I realize that people are going to judge me and have preconceived ideas about who I am. I understand that no matter what I do, the stereotypes of Black men will precede me and somehow I will have to prove myself over and over again. I know that people will be afraid of me, will think less of me, and will put the label of "Black" man on me, no matter what I do.

So as a Black man, what can I do? How do I deal with the multiplicity of challenges that I face on a daily basis? Do I throw my hands up in defeat and give up? Do I accept the stereotypes and become just another Black male statistic, thrown into the ever-increasing prison population? Do I succumb to the pressure and lose my identity and try to become someone that I'm not?

In order for me to deal with the aforementioned challenges, I choose to first and foremost see myself as a man, not just a Black man. If I see the world only through the lens of a Black man, I limit my perception of the world. When I let go of my attachment to being Black first, I open the door to infinite possibilities for myself as a human being. This is not a denial of my ethnicity; it is simply an affirmation of my true potential and my humanity. This awareness gives me an entirely new perspective on the world.

With this perspective, I can honestly say that I absolutely love being a Black man. I have come to this conclusion as a result of the past fifteen years of doing my emotional work and removing my shadows. I am now completely comfortable with who I am as a human being, and I recognize that I am a man who happens to be Black. I am proud of my racial heritage, but the true source of my power transcends the color of my skin.

When I view the world from this perspective, I begin to recognize that although there is ignorance and hatred in the world, racism in and of itself is actually an over-used word in our society that keeps us separate and in denial of our oneness. This does not excuse injustice and oppression for people of color; it simply acknowledges that racism is a disease of the mind. In objective scientific terms, it isn't real; it is a man made creation that exists only in our minds. I reflect over my personal mission statement: "As a man amongst men, I create a world of Love and understanding by loving myself and understanding others."

I fully grasp the implications of what these words mean to me. By loving myself and removing any blocks to my awareness, I am able to understand others without judgment. This allows me to constantly be in the moment without being attached to things that have happened to me in the past. By healing my anger and forgiving those who have hurt me, I can be fully present to people in my life;

therefore, I do not think in over generalized statements and use words and phrases like 'those white people' or 'them' and 'they'. I live in the moment and address each individual situation in the moment. This is the beauty of healing your heart. It frees you from your past and keeps you in the present moment.

My intention is for you to have a new perception about Black men after reading this article. The truth is, we are no different than any other group of men. We are loving, caring, compassionate, sensitive, intelligent, forgiving, and courageous. We love our country and our families. We deal with all of the same emotions and challenges as anyone else. We do not all blame society for our challenges, and we are constantly making positive contributions to America. We are definitely an asset to this country, not a liability.

I am reminded of a lesson I learned from Wayne Dyer, in which he taught me that I should never focus my attention on that which I am against; instead, I must focus my attention on that which I am for, and I will experience that as a result. So, instead of being against racism, I am for unity. Instead of taking a position against hatred, I take a stand for love.

As Dr. Martin Luther King, Jr., said: "We're afraid of each other because we do not know one another; we do not know one another because most of us are separated from each other." My intention is to remove the perceived separation and create oneness. This is the driving force in my life. I want to be the change I want to see in the world, and I invite you to join me in creating a world of love, peace, and unity.

In the immortal words of John Lennon: "You may say that I'm a dreamer, but I'm not the only one. I hope someday you'll join us, and the world will be as one."

Won't you join me?

Coach Michael Taylor

This article sums up my beliefs about what it means to be a Black man in America today. There will always be trials and triumphs, and it is our responsibility to embrace both. Despite all of the challenges, I believe we are poised to experience unprecedented levels of success now and in the future, and the reports of our demise are completely unwarranted.

The key is for us not to buy in to the negative media. We must understand and accept that the media's job is to always showcase what is wrong with the world. This is especially true when it comes to Black men. The media will showcase all of the negative stereotypes of Black men, but seldom will they show all of the amazing things that we have done. But the time has come for us not to place blame on the media, but to do our own research and find out the truth about who we are. It is now our responsibility to find the facts and not rely on the media for our information.

Few people have done this as effectively as filmmaker Janks Morton. (www.whatblackmenthink.com) Janks is the creator of two really powerful films that expose the lies perpetuated by our media about Black men. His first film was entitled "What Black Men Think" and was televised on the Documentary Channel, and his second film was entitled

"Hoodwinked", which expanded on the truths that he showcased in his first film.

One of the biggest myths and stereotypes that he dispelled in his film was this idea that there are more Black men in jail than there are in college. In my heart of hearts, I have always felt that this was true, but Mr. Morton provided the actual statistics to substantiate what I have always believed. The amazing thing about the film was how he asked college students if there were more Black men in prison than in college, and the overwhelming majority of them believed that jail was the correct answer.

According to Mr. Morton, in 2012 there were 823,000 Black men in jail and 1,444,979 Black men in college. While that is still a very high number of incarcerated men, the truth remains that there are a lot more Black men in college than in jail. He also substantiated that between the years 2000 and 2012, the incarceration rate rose less than 5 percent, while the percentage of Black men going to college rose by more than 75% in that same time frame. Have you ever seen these statistics in mainstream media?

This is the type of information we should be sharing with each other to empower ourselves to excel, but the truth of the matter is that there are a lot of Black people who actually attacked Mr. Morton and said that his data was incorrect. They accused him of skewing the data and not being honest, and they accused him of minimizing the plight of Black men.

Although I have not confirmed Mr. Morton's data, I agree with him 100%, and I support his work. I refuse to believe the negative media portrayal of Black men, and once again I state that Black men are not an endangered species.

I use my own research and observations to come to my own conclusions about the status of Black men in America, which is that we are definitely moving in the right direction despite obvious challenges in our communities.

So, I would like to challenge you right now to see if you are aware of the successes Black men are having right now. Have you ever heard of the following men:

Neale Degrasse Tyson
An American astrophysicist and science communicator. He is currently the Frederick P. Rose Director of the Hayden Planetarium at the Rose Center for Earth and Space and a research associate in the department of astrophysics at the American Museum of Natural History.

Darius Rucker
An American musician. He first gained fame as the lead singer and rhythm guitarist of the rock band Hootie & the Blowfish. In 2009, he became the first African American to win the New Artist Award from the Country Music Association and only the second African American to win any award from the association.

Phil Ivey
An American professional poker player who has won eight World Series of Poker bracelets, one World Poker Tour title, and appeared at nine World Poker Tour final tables.

Don Thompson
President and Chief Executive Officer of McDonald's Corporation (NYSE: MCD). Don Thompson leads the world's largest foodservice company. McDonald's serves nearly 69 million customers every day in 119 countries and employs more than 1.8 million people across the globe in corporate and restaurant positions.

Michael Beckwith
An American New Thought minister, author, and founder of the Agape International Spiritual Center in Culver City, California, a New Thought church with a congregation estimated in excess of 8,000 members.

Keith Black
An American neurosurgeon specializing in the treatment of brain tumors and a prolific campaigner for the funding of cancer treatment. He is chairman of the neurosurgery department and director of the Maxine Dunitz Neurosurgical Institute at Cedars-Sinai Medical Center in Los Angeles, California[1]

Charles Frank Bolden, Jr.
The current Administrator of NASA, a retired United States Marine Corps general, and former NASA astronaut.

These Black men confirm for me the fact that Black men are doing quite well in this country despite the negative media generated stereotypes. It shows the diversity in our abilities, and it showcases the fact that we do a lot more than just play sports, sing, and dance. I could add thousands of more names to the list, but I hope you get my point. And while I'm on the subject, let me include a gentleman by the name of **Barack Obama**, who just happens to be the President Of The United States Of America. Do I need to say anything more about the success of Black men in America?

So, if you are a man who happens to be Black, be sure not to buy in to the negative media. If you truly want to live an extraordinary life, you must make a conscious decision to do so, create a powerful vision for your life, and then be willing to do whatever it takes to manifest that vision. I have shared some examples of men who have lived their dreams; now it's up to you to live yours.

Just remember: Do Not Buy In To The Negative Media! You are responsible for your own destiny. No one or no thing can keep you from succeeding except yourself.

"Physical fitness is not only one of the most important keys to a healthy body, it is the basis of dynamic and creative intellectual activity."
John F. Kennedy

Key #7: Take Care Of Your Physical Body

When I was 18 years old, I received my first full-time job working as a salesman for a building supply retailer. I had always had a very strong work ethic, so being on time, working hard, and wanting to climb the corporate ladder seemed to be encoded in my DNA.

Although I was a very responsible employee that prided himself on never being late, I was still a teenager who wasn't quite ready to give up my partying life. I remember going out to the clubs and hanging out until 3 or 4 o'clock in the morning, driving home and sleeping for a couple hours, then showing up for work by 7:00 a.m. There were a few times when I even stayed up so late, I would sleep in my car in the parking lot at my job and get up to go to work.

One morning after staying up extremely late, I was in the shower, and as I lifted my arm I felt a really sharp pain in my chest. The pain immediately went away, so I disregarded it and headed for work.

Once I got to work, my job was to fill up a lumber rack with some 2X4's and make sure that all the other lumber racks were filled. As I began loading the 2X4's, I felt that sharp pain in my chest again. I disregarded the pain and continued what I was doing. After loading several of the 2X4's, all of a sudden I felt the most unbearable pain I had ever experienced. It felt as if someone had taken a 20-inch dagger and drove it through my heart. The entire left side of my body went numb, and the pain was so intense that I blacked out and fell to the floor.

When I woke up, there were people all around me. There were paramedics, my manager, my co-workers, and even customers all gathered around me, trying to see what had happened. The paramedics then put me on a stretcher and began rolling me outside to be placed in the ambulance. As they were rolling me through the store, I remember asking the guy if he would pull the sheet over my head because I was actually a little embarrassed.

As we were headed to the hospital with sirens blasting and the paramedics connecting me with IVs, I noticed that I was no longer in pain. I told the paramedics that I felt okay, and when he looked at my heart rate on the monitor, he mentioned that my heart seemed to be okay but that we obviously had to continue to go to the hospital for observation.

Once we got to the hospital, the nurses hooked me up with EKGs and heart monitors because it appeared that I had had a heart attack.

After approximately an hour, the doctor finally shows up and asks me what was wrong. I looked at him and said, "You're the doctor. You should be telling me what's wrong."

He then told me that he couldn't find anything wrong with my heart. As a matter of fact, he said that I was extremely healthy and that he couldn't figure out what had happened. He began asking me questions about my diet, if I drank alcohol, and if I had used any illegal drugs. When I answered no to all of these questions, he became perplexed. He then asked me if I had done anything out of the ordinary. I thought about it for a moment, then told him that I hadn't been sleeping much. He asked me why not, and I told him that I had been staying up pretty late and partying just a little too much.

When he finally coaxed me into telling him just how little I had been sleeping, he gave a sigh of relief and said he knew exactly what the problem was. Apparently, my body was so exhausted that it literally shut down so it could rest. My chest muscles were so fatigued that they cramped up around my heart and temporarily caused my heart to stop beating. It mimicked a heart attack, although it wasn't one.

The doctor then told me that all I needed to do was get some rest and I would be fine. He prescribed some muscle relaxers and sleeping pills, and once I got home, I slept for 32 hours.

After that ordeal, I had a new appreciation for my physical body. The fact that my body was smart enough to shut down because I wasn't taking care of it really changed my attitude about my body. Since that incident, I have always had a deep respect and admiration for my body, and I have not abused it since. I have been working out for approximately 30 years now, and I make sure that I refrain from alcohol, drugs, and overeating. I make sure that I get a physical every year, and I do my very best to maintain my health.

According to some statistics (I really dislike statistics, but this is important), Black men lead the nation in most health related illnesses and deaths. What we must do is make a commitment to taking better care of our bodies. I'd like to take this opportunity to share ten things Black men can do to take care of their physical bodies.

1. **Get an annual check up**.
   It is extremely important for men to get physical

exams. Men are hesitant to go to the doctor for myriad reasons, but the fact remains that getting a physical and early detection of illnesses improve your chances of overcoming those illnesses.

2. **Watch your diet.**
Yes, we love our soul food, and yes, we love to eat, but we must understand that there are certain foods that are detrimental to our bodies. Fried foods and high fat foods are the leading cause of weight gain and disease. Make a commitment to yourself to eat healthier, and minimize the amount of food you eat.

3. **Exercise**
You must understand that the human body is not designed to sit still; it is designed to move. It is the only thing on this planet that actually gets stronger the more you use it. Moderate exercise can extend your lifespan, help you lose weight, and help you ward off illnesses.

4. **Maintain a desirable weight.**
If you are overweight, make a commitment to drop some pounds. As you lose the weight, you receive lots of health benefits, as well as increased self-esteem.

5. **Limit your alcohol intake.**
Alcohol abuse leads to all sorts of health related illnesses. It also leads to depression. Be sure to reduce your alcohol intake, and by all means, never drink and drive.

6. **Stop smoking, and do not abuse illegal drugs.**
Enough said!

7. **Learn to relax.**
   There are several documented studies regarding the benefits of meditation. Learning to relax makes you more productive and focused, and it can help you eliminate the need for alcohol or drugs.

8. **Laugh often.**
   Its been said that people don't stop playing because they get old; they get old because they stop playing. Never stop playing! Make it a point to laugh and laugh often.

9. **Learn something new.**
   Learning should be a lifelong process. Studies have shown that people who keep learning throughout their lifetimes are less likely to experience Alzheimer's and dementia. Never stop learning!

10. **Volunteer.**
    Believe it or not, volunteering your time and talents to help other people can actually be good for your health. Studies have shown that people who help take care of others tend to be happier and healthier than those who don't.

These are ten things you can do to help you take care of your physical body. Taking care of your body can sometimes be a challenging thing, but it is important for you to make this a priority in your life.

Sadly, we lose too many men to preventable diseases simply because they refuse to get a check up. I understand how scary it can be to go see a doctor, but you must realize that early detection is the key to eradicating a lot of senseless deaths. In addition, we lose far too many men to alcohol related deaths that are easily prevented.

I would like to challenge you right now to take and moment and think about your own body. I'd like you to get a pen or pencil and do a simple exercise.

I want you to fill in the blanks:

If I would _____ right now, it would help me take care of my physical body.

I would like to _____ so that I will feel better about my body.

I am _____ pounds over my ideal weight.

I am committed to losing _____ pounds in 2013.

I am going to stop smoking, starting _____.

I am going to begin an exercise program _____.

I am going to make an appointment to see a doctor by _____.

The one thing that I do that I know isn't good for my health is _____.

In terms of my physical health, my goal for 2013 is to _____.

The one thing I can do right now to begin improving my health is _____ .

The one thing that scares me about my body is
_____ .

I am going to
_____ so that I can remove that fear.

The key is for you to begin doing something to improve your health. Use these questions as a starting point to get the ball rolling and to support you in taking care of your physical body.

Good luck!

*"Too many people spend money they haven't earned
to buy things they don't want to impress
people they don't like."*
Will Smith

Key #8: Manage Your Finances

I started my first company when I was 14 years old, even though at the time I didn't know that was what I was doing. I convinced the owner of a motorcycle shop to hire me to clean his garage for $5 an hour when the minimum wage was only $1.40 an hour.

When I first approached him about the job, he asked me why he should hire me, and I told him that I could clean and organize his garage in a way that would help him be better organized and make him more money. He asked me how much I would charge him, and I told him that I would clean his garage first, then he could decide how much my services were worth.

He agreed, and I cleaned his garage as if my life depended on it. When I finished, his garage was absolutely spotless. I did such a great job, even his mechanics insisted that he hire me. He then decided that $5 an hour was a fair wage, and I definitely agreed because I would have done it for $1 an hour; I just wanted a job.

After working there a few weeks, the owner began referring me to some of his friends that also owned garages, and before I knew it I had three paying clients.
I had my first taste of entrepreneurship, and I loved it! Since then, all I've ever dreamed of was owning my own company so I'm not surprised that I became an entrepreneur.

After that job, I began working in a grocery store. I started out as a sacker and worked my way up to stocker in a pretty short period of time. I was in high school now, and instead of playing sports, I decided that I wanted to learn about the business world. I began reading business books and listening to audio programs about becoming wealthy. I actually became obsessed with getting rich.

In order to make additional money, I took two of my passions, which were installing car stereos and listening to music, and turned them into businesses. I began installing car stereos for my friends, and I also became a disc jockey.

Being a DJ in high school was probably one of the coolest jobs a guy could have. I purchased my own equipment and would do parties and high school dances, which meant that I not only had access to the parties, but to lots of women as well. Life was good!

My most memorable moment as a DJ came about when I friend of mine called me to see if I was available to DJ a prom. Apparently, the band they had hired cancelled 2 days before the prom, and they were desperate for some music.

When the school coordinator called me and asked if I was available, I said yes. When she asked me what my fee was, I asked her how much they were going to pay the band. When she said $2000, I told her I could save her $500 because my fee was only $1500. She agreed, and I did the gig. The truth was, my fee was actually only $500, but I had learned the art of negotiation through some business books I had read, and that information paid off for me.

During my senior year in high school, I went to a seminar in which this salesman convinced me that I could become rich selling vacuum cleaners. I had already been bitten by the entrepreneurial bug, so when this guy told me that I could own my own business and make hundreds of thousands of dollars, I jumped at the opportunity.

Because of my previous experience in business, I felt confident that I could be successful. I knew I had the drive, the intelligence, the optimism, and the patience to succeed, so I took the risk and dropped out of high school to pursue my dream.

This was definitely not one of my best decisions. I failed miserably! Within six months, I never sold a single vacuum cleaner!

Fortunately for me, I was able to bounce back. As I mentioned in the previous chapters, I was eventually able to secure a great job, climb the corporate ladder, buy my first home at 23, and live the American Dream.

As I reflect back over my life, I realize that I have always been responsible when it comes to money. From a very young age, I took the time to understand how to make it and how to make it work for me. I definitely don't know everything about it, and I am constantly trying to learn more, but I wanted to share 10 things that I've learned about money that have helped me in my own life, and I believe they can be helpful to you.

1. **Your money does not define who you are!**

The first key that I shared with you if you want to live an extraordinary life is to "Know Thyself". If you fail to do this, then you will possibly get caught up in believing that your self worth is tied to how much money you make or how many material things you own. In our current masculine culture, we are taught that he who has the gold makes the rules, and therefore we do everything we can to try and get as much gold as possible.

In other words, we are constantly bombarded with images of nice homes, fancy cars, exotic vacations, fancy clothes and jewelry, and of course, beautiful women. As a result of taking in all of these images, we then create the subconscious belief that to be a man, we must have all of these things. This unconscious belief then begins to drive our behavior. We then buy nice cars that we really can't afford to try and impress our friends. We buy houses that are much bigger than we really need because we want to look successful. We go on fancy vacations to exotic places just to say we've been there and never truly experience the culture. We buy our kids expensive toys just to compete with our neighbors. And the list goes on and on.

The problem is, our self-esteem and self worth then become contingent upon our "stuff", and if we lose our stuff, we now have no sense of self worth.

Let me share my own experience.

As I mentioned previously, I have always been fairly successful in my life. I have always been a highly motivated, ambitious person with lots of goals and the ability to accomplish those goals. It wasn't until I went on my inner journey of self discovery that I realized what was actually driving my success.

As a result of doing my inner work and learning to Know Thyself, I discovered that I was actually driven by deep feelings of shame and inadequacy. I had such low self-esteem that I needed to accomplish things to feel good about myself. I learned that I had an insatiable need for approval, and by being successful, it made me look good and caused people to like me.

This took rigorous honesty on my part and was a difficult

pill to swallow at the beginning. It took an incredible amount of vulnerability and emotional honesty to come to this realization, but once I acknowledged it head on, I gained my personal power back. By being completely honest with myself, I was able to stop pretending and get real with myself. In doing so, I became emotionally and psychologically free.

No longer did I have to hide behind my money, material things, titles, or accomplishments. I learned to be completely comfortable in my own skin, and I didn't need anything outside of myself to be accepted. In other words, I learned to love myself just as I am.

This can be extremely difficult for men because we get trapped in the illusion that we must have external things to be happy, but until we learn how to do this, no amount of money, sex, drugs, titles, or material possessions will satisfy us.

I'd like for you to take a moment and answer these questions honestly to yourself.

Have you ever felt alone and empty even when you've had all the external things society says you're supposed to have?

Have you ever felt like an ATM machine to your wife or girlfriend because they are always draining you of cash?

Do you currently drive a car that you know you really can't afford?

Are you currently drowning in debt and have been too afraid to tell anyone or do anything about it?

Have you ever felt that people wouldn't truly accept you if you didn't have lots of "stuff"?

Are you uncomfortable dating someone who makes more money than you, and you feel threatened by it?

Take a moment and be completely honest with yourself. Being honest with yourself is the first step to change, so do not be afraid to do so.

If you answered yes to any of these questions, there is a good possibility that you have allowed your money to define you. The time has come for you to get real with yourself and follow the first key to living an extraordinary life.

Know Thyself!

This means that it is time for you to become self-introspective and figure out how to love yourself. Until you do this, your life will never be extraordinary.

2. **You must be willing to examine your beliefs about money!**

It is important for you to be completely honest with yourself about your beliefs around money. A lot of people have hidden subconscious beliefs about money that will ultimately sabotage their ability to create money in their own lives. Take a look at this list of some limiting beliefs people have about money and see if you relate to any of them.

1. Money is the root of all evil (The actual quote is "The love of money is the root of all evil").
2. I don't deserve to have a lot of money.

3. There is not enough money to go around.
4. If I have a little more than I need to get by, someone else has to go without.
5. If I am successful, people will hate me.
6. If I make a lot of money, I will be betraying my father, who never made much money.
7. The rich get richer.
8. The poor get poorer.
9. Money is hard to deal with.
10. Money is hard to get.
11. You have to work hard to get it
12. To save money, you have to do without things.
13. Time is money.
14. I can't have money and free time.
15. Money is not spiritual.
16. You have to do lots of things you don't like in order to have money.
17. I do not have enough to share or give away.
18. Having money stops you from being happy.
19. Money spoils you.

(List compiled from www.mandyevans.com)

As you're reading this list, simply notice if any of these beliefs resonate with you. Do you remember your parents saying any of them? Have you ever said any of them to other people? Do you believe any of them?

Your ability to make money is directly linked to your beliefs about money. If you are not making the amount of money you would like to make, you must first uncover your hidden beliefs about money and change them. Once you do, you open the door to creating any amount of money that you'd like.

3. **Expect the unexpected**

It's impossible to know exactly what is going to happen in your life. The key to dealing with adversity is to Know Thyself, which gives you the ability to deal with whatever life throws at you. When I went through my divorce, I had no way of knowing how financially devastating it would be. Losing everything, including my family and all of my financial assets, was extremely difficult. I didn't expect it, but it happened.

In retrospect, I can now see how my divorce was the best thing that could have happened to me. It caused me to "wake up" and discover who I really was. If not for my divorce, I would probably still be stuck on that societal roller coaster, doing everything society said I was supposed to do to be happy. Because of the unexpected, I was propelled to get out of my comfort zone and become a writer and speaker and live the life I've always dreamed of.

4. **Pay Yourself First**

Managing your finances means that you make a commitment to understanding how much money is coming in and how much money is going out. The surefire way of knowing this is by having a budget. Having a budget means you become willing to sit down and write exactly what's coming in and what's going out. As simplistic as this sounds, most people are not willing to do this, then they wonder why their finances are out of control.

Once you establish your budget, you must learn to pay yourself first as part of your budget. This can be extremely difficult if you're drowning in debt, but the key to your financial success lies within your ability to pay yourself first. In other words, you simply make a commitment to saving some money every month. If you look at it as paying yourself first each month, it makes it a little easier to make the commitment.

The key is to simply begin. You can start by committing to saving a minimal amount of money each month. You get to decide how much, but you must be willing to save the same amount each and every month. Once you do it for several months, you will begin to feel good about it, and then you will want to increase it. Pretty soon it will become a habit, and you will be on your way to improving your finances.

5. How Much You Spend Is More Important Than How Much You Make

I used to believe that I needed to make at least $100K per year to be happy. In my mind, that was the true gauge of success. But I can now say that a person can make $7K per year (or less) and still be happy.

How can I say this? Because I've done it!

When I went through my bankruptcy and lost everything, I couldn't find a job for approximately 2 years. During this time, I was deeply involved in Knowing Thyself and was absolutely committed to learning how to be authentically happy. As a result of all of the transformational work I participated in, I got to a place where I was completely happy with who I was as a man. I no longer needed external validation, and I experienced life's ultimate paradox: I had absolutely nothing and absolutely everything at the same time. Although I had very few material things, I had everything I needed, which was the inner peace and joy that I had begun to experience as a result of my inner work.

What I learned from this experience was that how much I spent was more important than how much I made. So, I simply learned how to spend less, which then resulted in me needing to make less. I was making less money than I ever had, and paradoxically, I was happier than I'd ever been.

6. Maintain Good Credit

In today's economy, having good credit is mandatory. The secret is not to become dependent on them, but it is important to have them. After my divorce, I watched my credit score plunge, and it took me several years to rebuild it. But I stuck with it and eventually got my score back up to an excellent rating. The key was to minimize my spending and always pay my balances at the end of the month.

If you truly want to manage your finances, maintaining a good credit score is a great place to start.

7. Invest In Your Financial Literacy

With all of the information available to everyone these days, there is no excuse not to invest in your financial literacy, which simply means you learn some basic things about budgeting, saving, and investing. It is your responsibility to understand how your retirement plan works, what to expect from Social Security, what your health care plan provides, and whether or not you will be able to retire comfortably. You must learn about credit card rates and fees and figure out which card works best for your situation.

There are always ways to learn these things; you simply must make the commitment to do so. You can start by searching the Internet or going to the library or your bank to gain the knowledge to make good financial decisions. No one can do this for you, but you can get support to help you.

Invest in your financial literacy today to comfortably manage your finances tomorrow.

8. It's Not About The Stuff

If you really stop and think deeply about this, you may notice that everything we do, we do to experience a feeling. The driving force for most of us is to feel good. We buy food to feel good, we buy clothes to feel good, we buy cars to feel good, and the list goes on and on. But have you noticed just how quickly those good feelings go away after you purchase something? Have you ever wondered why that is?

The answer is, it's not about the stuff; it's about the feeling. If we learn how to feel good without the stuff, then we can become genuinely happy without it. Managing your finances actually begins with knowing how you feel. If you are lonely and depressed, you will possibly spend money to avoid feeling that way. If you lack confidence and self-esteem, you will try to compensate for that through materialism and spending.

So, be sure to take some time to Know Thyself and come to the understanding that it's not about the stuff; it's about your feelings. When you truly understand this, you can have as much stuff as you want.

9. Money Is Spiritual

If you have the belief that money is the root of all evil or that money is bad, then the time has come for you to change that belief. Money isn't good or bad; it is simply a form of energy and exchange. How it is used will determine whether it does good things or bad things in your life or in the world.

It is my fervent belief that there is absolutely nothing wrong with making money, and lots of it. If you happen to be religious and believe in God, then making money could simply allow you to use it to serve your God. Just imagine how much good you could do for your God if you were a billionaire versus being poor. You could definitely feed more people and change the world with a fat bank account versus an empty one.

I also believe that there are Universal laws and principles that govern the Universe, and when you learn how those laws work, you can use them for your highest good to manifest any amount of money that you want.

One of those laws is called the law of attraction. In its simplest form, it states that everything is energy, and since everything is energy, all you have to do is put yourself in the same vibrational energy field of what you want. and you can attract it into your life.

Albert Einstein said it this way:

"Everything is energy, that's just the way that it is. Match the frequency of the reality that you want to create, and there is no way that you cannot create that reality. It can be no other way. This isn't philosophy; this is physics."

If you accept this theory, then spirituality takes on a whole new meaning because if everything is energy, then the highest form of energy would be spirit; therefore, money is spiritual.

10. Give Something Back

It's been said that "To whom much is given, much is expected." If you are blessed with financial abundance, then a way to acknowledge that abundance is to give some away. There is a law that is called the law of reciprocity, which basically means what you put out will come back to you or be reciprocated. When you give love, you receive love. When you share kindness, you receive kindness. When you give money, you receive money. This is a universal law that works every time, but you have to believe and trust in it to have it work for you.

The best way to do this is to give with an open heart without any expectation of return. If you give some money, don't think in the back of your mind, *I'm going to get some money back*. Simply count your blessings that you have it to give away and be grateful that you were able to help someone less fortunate than you. When you surrender to this law, the Universe will bless you in countless ways, and your blessings will be overflowing. Even if you only have a dollar to give, if you do it with an open heart and an open mind, you will be blessed immeasurably.

Always remember to give something back!

"One machine can do the work of fifty ordinary men. No machine can do the work of one extraordinary man."
Elbert Hubbard

Key #9: Embrace Technology

If I had to choose two words that explain why I am so optimistic about the future, those words would be 'technology' and 'information'. For me, these two words are the keys for anyone who is committed to living an extraordinary life.

Let me explain why I feel this way.

It wasn't that long ago in our country's history when the primary source of jobs was manufacturing. For a lot of men, this meant working in factories or coal mines, which didn't take a lot of formal education or training, but it allowed a man to make a decent living.

Over the past 25 years or so, something amazing began to happen. We entered into the information and technology age, and all of a sudden machines began doing the work that a lot of men were accustomed to doing. As a result, unskilled labor was transformed because now a man had to learn how to use technology in order to secure good paying jobs. He could no longer rely just on his hands to make money; he had to rely on his brain as well. This meant that he now had to learn how to use computers and advanced technology if he really wanted to keep up with the high paying jobs.

As this information age continued to progress, technology began changing a lot of other industries. For example, there was a time when the secretary who could type the fastest was the one who would make the most money. But with the advancement of technology and the elimination of typewriters, the secretary who could learn the latest computer software the fastest was the one who would be promoted quicker and receive the highest wages.

So all of a sudden, your ability to earn was directly linked to your ability to learn.

In computer technology, there is an interesting theory called Moore's Law. This law states that the processor speeds or overall processing power for computers will double every two years. A quick check among technicians in different computer companies shows that the term is not very popular, but the rule is still accepted.

The point is, technology moves at an incredibly fast speed, and I believe that the people who are willing to embrace technology and keep pace with it will be the people who truly succeed in this fast-paced, technology driven information age we now live in.

To give you some example of this, I'd like to share a couple stories from my own life that demonstrate what I'm talking about.

A couple years ago, the company that I work for had a consultant come in and give them a quote to put together an introductory video for newly hired employees. It just so happened that one of the owners of the company and I had a very good relationship, and he told me about the consultation. When I asked him how much the company was going to charge to put together the video, he said between $8-$10 thousand dollars.

They decided that the price was too high and declined the company's offer.

A couple weeks later, I purchased a new computer for my home office, and I was playing around with some video editing software that it came with and realized that I could actually make the introductory video for the company. I approached the owner about the project and asked him if he would be willing to pay me to make the video.

He asked me how much I would charge for it, and I told him that once I completed the video, if he liked it, then he could tell me how much he thought it was worth. If he didn't like it, he would not have to pay for it.

Since it was a no-lose proposition for him, he agreed, and I began working on the video.

The important lesson that I want to share here is the fact that I didn't even know how to use the software before I committed to making the video. By making the commitment to make the video, I now had to learn how to use it.

In my mind, I was actually getting paid to do something that I loved to do. Learning how to use my new computer and software wasn't work to me. It was fun! And now I was going to get paid for having fun. How cool was that?

It took me approximately 5 hours to write the script, 2 hours to record some video. and 12 hours of editing and finalizing the video. When I finished and presented it to the owner, he was blown away. He absolutely loved it!

When he asked me how much he owed me, I asked him how much he thought it was worth. Since I had had so much fun making it and learning how to use my computer, I figured I'd be pretty happy if I made $500 on the project. The truth was, I didn't know how much it was actually worth. He thought about it for a moment, and then asked me if $1500 dollars was enough.

To say I was excited would be a gross understatement. I was way beyond excited, but I kept my composure and said that I believed that was a fair price. The truth was, he probably would have paid me more if I would have asked, but this was way more than I had anticipated.

As a result of my willingness to embrace technology, I actually earned enough money to pay for my computer.

Another example of the importance of technology and information occurred when I decided that I wanted to learn how to use green screen technology on my computer. This is the same technology that filmmakers use when they make movies. It works like this: you record your video using a green background. Once you've recorded it, you can then use your computer to remove the green background and replace it with any other background that you like. For example, I could shoot a video on green screen, and then I could replace the green screen background with a waterfall scene of a scenic mountain scene or a floating-in-space scene. Get the picture?

So, I decided I wanted to learn how to do this, and I signed up for a class at a local learning center. The cost of the class was $149. I thought that was a pretty minimal charge, considering that I would be using it a lot in my business, so cost really wasn't an issue.

A few days before I was scheduled to take the class, I decided to do an Internet search about the technology to give me a head start before I went to the class. During my search, I came across a video in which these two young kids, who couldn't have been more than 15 years old, had posted a video on the Internet on how to use green screen technology. Amazingly, after watching their fifteen-minute video, I learned everything I needed to know about green screen technology - and it didn't cost me anything! Not a single penny! I canceled my class and saved myself $149.

The point, once again, is if you are committed to living an extraordinary life, you must embrace technology and be willing to absorb lots of information. Know that you have an infinite capacity for learning if you will simply commit to never stop learning.

This does not mean that you have to become a computer or technology geek; it simply means that you are open to learning new things that are applicable to your life and can help improve the quality of your life.

Alvin Toffler said this: "The functional illiterate of the 21st Century will not be those who cannot read or write. It will be those who cannot learn, unlearn, and relearn."

Within our current information-driven society, those of us who are willing to learn, unlearn, and relearn are the ones who will experience phenomenal success in the future. The great thing about technology and information is that they are completely unbiased. They don't care if you're Black or white, young or old, rich or poor. They are at the beck and call of any human being who is willing to embrace them and take advantage of them.

So what about you? Are you ready and willing to embrace technology and allow it to enhance your life? Are you ready to learn, unlearn, and relearn so that you can live the life of your dreams while making a positive impact on the world?

If the answer is yes, then allow me to share 5 technologies that you must embrace if you're committed to living an extraordinary life.

1. **Computers / Tablets**
The driving force of technology is computers. Computers have equalized the playing field for anyone who is willing to learn. As the technology continues to increase and the prices continue to decrease, there is no excuse for anyone not to take advantage of computer technology. If you aren't using computers, make a commitment to take a class to learn how. It will open up a whole new world you may not have known existed.

2. **The Internet**
This is the holy grail of information. It is an infinite supply of information that can provide you with everything you need to accomplish anything you want. The Internet removes all boundaries from around the globe. Now you can connect with anyone in any place at anytime, simply through the Internet.

If you're not aware of this fact, you can find absolutely anything you're looking for on the Internet.

3. **Smartphones**
Smartphones are simply miniaturized computers. The advantage they have is mobility. With a smartphone, you can make calls, surf the Internet, check emails, send text messages, and basically do anything you can do with a full-size computer. The only real difference is the smaller screen. Each new generation of smartphones continues to get smaller and more powerful. Be sure to utilize their features because they do much, much more than just reach out and touch someone through the telephone.

4. Social Media
Social media is where people connect and interact with other people on the Internet. It is a wonderful way to keep in touch with family or friends or to join groups of like-minded people to support a specific cause. Companies like Facebook, Twitter, YouTube, Pinterest, and LinkedIn are great resources for you to connect with people around the globe or around the corner.

5. Software/Apps
Would you like to learn how to speak a new language or find a new recipe? Or maybe you'd like to find the best places to eat in the city that you live in? No matter what it is you would like to learn, there's an app for that. An app is a piece of software on your computer or smartphone that teaches you how to do something. Currently, there are nearly a million different apps available to teach you how to do just about anything. If you're willing to learn how to do something, all you have to do is download the app and get started. The really good news is that most of them are relatively cheap and give you a great amount of value if you're truly willing to learn how to use them. You can skip the classroom and go straight to the app and learn just about anything.

In summary, if you are truly committed to living the life of your dreams, you must embrace technology and information. The key is to keep an open mind and be willing to learn, unlearn, and relearn. There is no one or no thing that can keep you from succeeding except yourself. By embracing these two key elements, you position yourself for unlimited success in all areas of your life.

I wanted to close by sharing a few of the ways I have used technology to live my dreams. Obviously, your life is probably a lot different from mine, but I think you will be able to see some benefits that you can apply to your own lives through my sharing.

First of all, I am writing this book on the computer that I mentioned at the beginning of this chapter. I absolutely love technology, and I am always looking for ways to learn more about it. By embracing technology and learning how to use the word processing program on my computer, I am able to express my creativity by writing books, blog posts, and articles.

Secondly, I currently host and maintain my own websites for my business. Because of my love of technology and my willingness to learn how to use it, I save myself literally thousands of dollars a year by being able to do most of this myself.

Check them out here:
www.coachmichaeltaylor.com
www.creationpublishing.com
www.anewconversationwithmen.com

Thirdly, I am launching my own publishing company from the comfort of my own home. Because of technology, I am building my media empire from my home office. I have distribution channels for my books and products and can now ship them anywhere in the world. This would not have been possible just ten years ago without having to have lots of employees and office space. Technology allows me to do this with a single employee.

Fourth, I currently host an online radio show that can be listened to anywhere in the world. Technology allows me to reach people anywhere with my message and my products. I currently receive approximately 1000 downloads of my radio show every month, and I have listeners from all corners of the globe.

Fifth, I am launching a new television talk show in February 2013 on a Houston Public TV Channel. This would not be possible without my knowledge of computers and the Internet. It is also made possible by my willingness to learn how to become a videographer and TV show producer.

I share these things not to brag, but to inspire you. If I can accomplish all of these things with very limited education and money, but a willingness to learn new things, I know you can also.

I can attribute all of my success to my confidence in myself and my willingness to learn new things. If I can do it, I know that you can, too.

Remember, never stop learning, and be sure to embrace technology to live the life of your dreams.

Good luck!

*"Service to others is the rent you pay for
your room here on Earth."*
Muhammad Ali

Key #10: Be In Service To Your Community

It is my contention that every human being has a divine purpose. I also believe that we show up with everything we need in order to fulfill that purpose; unfortunately, most people do not find nor fulfill their purpose because we live in a world that constantly tells us to "look outside" of ourselves for happiness and fulfillment.

In other words, we pursue external things like money, cars, titles, sex, work, and relationships because we believe these things will make us happy and provide security. Our focus is always "out there" instead of "in here".

Probably the most difficult thing we will ever do is to change our focus and become self-introspective, which means taking a look within our own hearts and minds to discover who we really are and why we are here. It isn't until we make a commitment to do this that we can find true fulfillment, passion, and purpose.

For those who follow the Christian religion, you may recall Jesus saying, "Seek ye first the kingdom of Heaven, and all things will be given unto you." He then clarified what he meant by saying, "The kingdom of Heaven does not come from your careful observation. You can not say here it is or there it is because the kingdom of Heaven is within you!"

The kingdom of Heaven is within you, and it is your responsibility to enter that kingdom and find your passion and your purpose.

So how does a person find their purpose?

Earlier in this book, I invited you to Know Thyself. This is the key to finding your purpose. Before you do anything else, you must take this first step. Knowing thyself means that you fully understand who you are as a human being. It means understanding your strengths and weaknesses, it means knowing your values, it means knowing what you truly believe about yourself about life and about the world around you. It is about knowing how you feel and being able to express your feelings. It is about facing your fears and being willing to do whatever it takes to move through them.

It is an inner journey that few people will take, but if you're reading this right now, you are one of those few people.

Once you Know Thyself, there are two things you have to do to find your purpose.

1. You must discover your passion and the things you love to do.
2. You must apply your passions to help make the world a better place.

To help you discover your passions, I want you to take a moment and ask yourself what are some of the things you love to do. It could be writing or speaking, or maybe it could be cooking or working on cars. Only you can know what you love to do, so take a moment and think about it.

If you're not sure what you really love to do, let me share three ways to know when you're doing what you love. The first way to know if you're doing what you love is that when you're doing it, time literally disappears. For example, I love writing. When I'm writing, I can be at my computer for eight to ten hours, and I promise you it feels like 20 minutes. Time literally disappears when I'm writing. So think about something you do, and while you're doing it you lose track of time. This is the first way to know when you are doing what you love.

The second way to know is that you will do it without the thought of compensation. In other words, you simply do it because you love doing it, and it doesn't matter if you get paid for doing it. Doing it brings you joy and lights you up.

This does not mean that you can't or shouldn't get paid to do it; on the contrary, when you are doing what you truly love, in a lot of cases you should be compensated handsomely for your work. But the fact remains, if you truly love to do something, you will do it even if you never get paid.

The third way of knowing is that you want to share what you do with others. When you take what you love and share it with others, it warms your heart and gives you a sense of meaning and purpose. It doesn't matter what it is you're doing; what matters is that you love doing it.

Whenever I write a book, I can't wait to share it with others. I love the creative process of writing it, and I love the benefits that my readers receive from reading it. Even if I never sold a book, I would still write simply because I love doing it. But when I'm able to share my writings with others and I know that my words have positively impacted someone's life in a positive way, I am fulfilled and happy because I have shared what I love doing with others.

Your challenge is to find out what you love to do.

Once you've found out, then the next step is to take what you love to do and figure out a way to help or serve others. For example, I love writing. By sharing my knowledge with others through my books, I am serving others by inspiring them to reach their full potential. So I take my passion, which is writing, then I share my writing with others to help improve their lives, and in doing so I am making the world a better place.

So, Passion + Service = Purpose

It's simple, but not easy. But I can assure you that it is doable for you.

You must understand that there is no purpose that is bigger or better than another purpose. There is only "your" purpose. Do not try and compare yourself to others. Find out what you love to do, serve others, and you will fulfill your purpose.

Another way to find your purpose is to simply begin doing something that helps other people. For example, you could go to a homeless shelter and help serve food. While you're there, you may find out that you love serving food, and that could become your purpose.

Or maybe you could mentor a child and help them stay on the right track, and then you find out that you love teaching, and that could be your purpose.

What if you went to an old folks home and spent some time with someone who has no family and would simply love some company? Could your purpose be counseling and consoling others?

Or maybe there is a family member or a co-worker who has been struggling financially, and you know that you could support them in some way with some financial support. Your purpose could be giving.

Do you know how to fix cars or repair homes and could share that knowledge with someone? Your purpose could be sharing your expertise.

Could you take three hours a week and go to an elementary school and read to young children? Your purpose could be found in that elementary school.

There are literally thousands of things you can be doing right now to serve your community. It's time for you to find your passion and your purpose.

What the world needs right now are people who are willing to be in service to humanity. The world is crying out for positive voices who are committed to making the world a better place.

As men who happen to be Black, we have an excellent opportunity to allow our voices to be heard and encourage others to live extraordinary lives. No longer can we play victims and wait for others to help us resolve our problems. It's up to us now, and my hope is that this book has inspired you to take positive action.

I know without question that every man has the capacity to live an extraordinary life, and Black men are no different than any other men. What has been missing are the resources to support them in reaching their full potential, and I have made it my life's work to provide some of those resources.

I want to close by thanking you for taking the time to read this book. Now the real work begins. You must apply what you have learned to your own life and commit to making it extraordinary. Once you do, reach one and teach one and pass it on.

Always remember that Black men are not an endangered species, and the way to ensure that is by you living an extraordinary life.

Good luck!

Coach Michael Taylor

About The Author

Michael Taylor is President and CEO of Creation Publishing Group. He is an author, Life Coach and radio show host who has dedicated his life to empowering men to reach their full potential. He has studied and researched men's issues for the past twenty years and has inspired thousands of men through his books, seminars and radio programs.

When he is not running his company you will find him hanging out with his wife at the movies or being a father to his three grown children. He considers himself to be an irrepressible optimist with a passion for the impossible and he enjoys writing, public speaking and computers.

www.ingramcontent.com/pod-product-compliance
Lightning Source LLC
Chambersburg PA
CBHW072336300426
44109CB00042B/1643